Pretenders to the Throne

Pretenders to the Throne

The Consumer Movement in the United States

Lucy Black Creighton
Colorado Women's College

Lexington Books
D.C. Heath and Company
Lexington, Massachusetts
Toronto   London

Library of Congress Cataloging in Publication Data

Creighton, Lucy Black.
    Pretenders to the throne.

    Bibliography: p.
    Includes index.
    1. Consumer protection—United States. 2. Consumer education—
United States. I. Title. HC110.C63C73   381'.3   75-17334
ISBN 0-669-00085-X

Published simultaneously in Canada

Printed in the United States of America

International Standard Book Number: 0-669-00085-X

Library of Congress Catalog Card Number: 75-17334

To
Ann and Virginia

Contents

Preface

One of the pleasant uses of a preface is the chance to touch on matters that are inappropriate in the objective and impersonal context of the book itself. After the long months of writing the book, writing the Preface is a sign that the task is nearly at an end and that one has the opportunity to address the reader directly rather than through the medium of the subject matter.

Just as women have traditionally taken the role of consumers, women economists, more than men, have worked in the field of consumption economics. Whether this is because male economists have disdained the field and relegated it to women or because somehow women, more than men, have understood the symbiotic relation between consumption and the lives people lead need not be argued. At a time when there has come to be less and less role assignment on the basis of sex, women are not bound by former divisions of labor, and men are beginning to see the importance of analyzing what was formerly thought of as the mundane and unimaginative task of being a "consumer."

My own interest in the subject of consumers grew out of graduate courses in microeconomic theory where I sensed, rather than knew, that the accepted theory of consumer demand did little to explain why people bought the particular goods they did. In developing a doctoral dissertation, I first tried to challenge the entire theory of demand. It was only after several abortive attempts in that direction that I turned to the consumer movement as a related, but more manageable, subject. In a gratifying way, however, the study of the consumer movement took me back to the classical theory of demand and provided me the opportunity to air some of my criticisms. I do not see this study of the consumer movement as an indictment of those who have worked in the consumer's interest. I see it rather as one more piece of evidence that economics needs a theory of consumption that will explain the relationship between the material goods and services people work for and their sense of individual and social well-being. My study has not led me to such a theory, but I will have accomplished my purpose if the study helps to point the way for someone else.

Writing a book is a tedious and often lonely process, and, at its conclusion I have come to realize that the phrase "without whose help" cannot be overused. I want to express my thanks to my colleagues Carolyn Bell and Sally Geis for their continuing encouragement of my professional work. I owe special thanks to Amy Pulver and to Winifred Creighton for their capable assistance with the mechanics of the manuscript. I acknowledge the useful (and sometimes painful) suggestions and criticisms of my economist son, Tom. Finally, to my husband I pay tribute for his incisive and careful editing of my writing and for his never-failing enthusiasm for my endeavors.

L.B.C.

Pretenders to the Throne

1

Introduction

Consumption is the sole end and purpose of all production; and the interest of the producer ought to be attended to only so far as it may be necessary for promoting that of the consumer.

Adam Smith, *The Wealth of Nations*

A growing recognition of consumers and consumer problems in the American economy has developed during recent years. Consumer advocates in both national and state governments call for more consumer protection and information. Across the country the consumer is the subject of an increasing amount of legislative and executive activity. Ralph Nader sees the consumer's problem as the epitome of the plight of the individual citizen in a society dominated by the large corporate bureaucracies of both business and government and calls for the dissolution of this power. Opponents of the new "consumerism" see the protection and promotion of consumers as one more example of growing government regulation, control of business and the decline of individual freedom and responsibility. In reply, consumer advocates contrast the political weakness of unorganized consumers with the political pressure that business or labor or agriculture can bring to bear on its own behalf.

Much of what is being said and done today recalls similar activity of nearly fifty years ago. Beginning in the late 1920s, a consumer movement,[a] in the name of "consumer sovereignty," sought to promote the position and authority of the consumer as a means to "raising the standard of living" for all consumers.[1]

The movement sought to assert the preeminence of consumers in the American economy. The position the consumer movement took was that the best interests of the consumer were guaranteed by the operation of competitive markets that made available at the lowest prices the goods that consumers wanted to buy. Consumers were thus the "sovereigns" of the economy. On such a basis, the consumer movement maintained, in Adam Smith's words, that "consumption is the sole end and purpose of all production; and the interest

---

[a]The consumer movement is defined here as the sum of the efforts of various individuals and groups identified with working for and promoting the interest of the consumer. By this definition, not only consumer organizations and consumer advocates but government promotion of the consumer, consumer education, and even business and labor activity on behalf of the consumer all become a part of the consumer movement.

1

of the producer ought to be attended to only so far as it may be necessary for promoting that of the consumer." Underlying this concern for the economic supremacy of the consumer was a belief on the part of those in the consumer movement that the level of consumption, and thus the level of consumer satisfaction or welfare, could be raised if the interest of consumers were the primary consideration in the economy.

Spokesmen for the consumer movement believed that, in fact, the American economy was directed toward the interests of producers rather than of consumers. They cited as evidence the increasing amount of advertising, the lack of consumer information about goods, the provision of government services to producers but not to consumers, and the increasing concentration of production and marketing services that limited the protection available to consumers through competitive markets. The consumer movement sought—through consumer organization, consumer representation in government, and consumer education—to establish the sovereignty of the consumer in the American economy.

This early consumer movement reached its height during the years of the Great Depression. Consumer testing services were organized, there were consumer advisors, or representatives, in several of the New Deal recovery programs, and a number of nationally organized women's groups identified themselves as part of the consumer movement. In addition, considerable interest in consumer education developed as one means of asserting consumer sovereignty; people would be taught in the public schools, as well as through adult groups, to be responsible and effective consumers. Critics, on the other hand, accused the consumer movement of wanting to substitute government regulation for the traditional American freedom of choice, and business saw the movement as a threat to its own interests. Yet for all its activities, the consumer movement's only real achievement was the passage of the 1938 Food, Drug, and Cosmetic Act that updated the 1906 law and established the Food and Drug Administration in the Department of Agriculture. During World War II support for the movement declined, and after the end of the war this support almost disappeared.

Beginning in about 1960, there began to be a renewed interest in consumers and their problems. As earlier, the interest derived from the belief that consumers are economically disadvantaged through lack of information in making competent judgments about the goods they buy and through lack of competition in the production and marketing of consumer goods. Recently, however, the strength of the consumer movement has come, not from governmental consumer representation or women's groups or education, but primarily from advocacy within both the federal and state governments, from organized labor, and from the extraordinary efforts of Ralph Nader. The result of this advocacy has been an increasing amount of consumer legislation proposed, debated, and passed by Congress. The executive branch as well has supported the consumer's cause. Nearly all the states have enacted broad consumer-protection measures.

Again, however, as in the thirties, there is no evidence that this action on behalf of consumers has brought about much change in the economic status of the consumer or aroused significant numbers of consumers to organize in their own behalf.

A study of these periods of activity in the consumer movement can give some clue to the movement's future course of development. But, more important, such a study can show the relationship between the consumer movement and economic theory that is fundamental to understanding the past and future of the consumer movement. This relationship suggests, in turn, some of the limitations of the present-day theory of consumption.

The goals of the consumer movement have derived from the concepts of *consumer* and *consumption* as they are defined in the economic theory of demand or consumer behavior. The concern for the consumer has been based on the proposition that the consumer's actual role in the.economy is something less than what economic theory says it should be. The work of the consumer movement has centered on furthering the economic interest—the sovereignty—of the rational consumer in competitive markets. An analysis of this work, however, suggests that to the extent that its economic theory is inconsistent with the realities of the modern economy and its consumers, a consumer movement based on such a theory has failed to reach its goals.

In the context of the consumer movement, the assumptions of the classical theory of consumer behavior are excessively limiting. Within the bounds of economic theory, to criticize the assumptions of rational behavior and utility-maximization on the part of the consumer as "unreal" is pointless because in general equilibrium theory such behavior is a necessary condition for the optimum allocation of resources.[2] Yet these assumptions, when applied by the consumer movement to American consumers, are unsatisfactory for the analysis of modern consumption patterns. Similarly, in assuming competitive markets as a necessary condition for the realization of the consumer's interest, the consumer movement puts itself in the position of seeking the impossible. But because there is no other accepted definition of the consumer interest in the United States (a point to be discussed more fully in Chapter 7), the consumer movement has taken the role of the consumer as it stands in classical economic analysis and defined itself and its purposes in such economic terms.

The thesis of this study of the consumer movement is that much of the failure of the consumer movement, both in organizing consumers and in bringing about changes in the economy that would assert the sovereignty of the consumer, can be explained by the fact that the consumer movement has been based on the classical microeconomic theory of the rational consumer operating in competitive markets. But this view, which puts the consumer in the best possible place in the economic scheme of things, does not harmonize with the reality of modern American consumption. In two important respects reliance on this view of the consumer's role in the economy has hampered the consumer movement in its efforts to establish consumer sovereignty and thus to improve consumer welfare.

First, in appealing to consumers, the consumer movement has been bound to the concept of the rational consumer, balancing expenditure against gain, and always looking for "his money's worth." To this end, the consumer movement has called for the dissemination of information about quantity, quality, and price that would enable consumers to make a determination of their "best buy." The consumer movement has pictured the wide choice of goods available to consumers as a problem for consumers rather than as an increase in consumer welfare. Yet the American consumer has an increasingly higher income and lives in an atmosphere that places a premium on spending for its own sake and that accords status to those who can spend without reference to cost. He also sees himself living in a country whose consumers are the envy of the world. Thus most American consumers do not identify themselves with the consumer of the consumer movement and, consequently, do not respond to the urgings for consumer organization for action in their own behalf.

Second, in working through government regulation for changes in the economy, the consumer movement has been bound to a definition of the consumer interest that is limited to rational consumers operating in competitive markets. This means that this interest can be fulfilled only where consumers are rational and markets are competitive. Since in the context of the contemporary American economy neither of these conditions appears possible, the consumer movement's goals of consumer sovereignty is unattainable through legislation and government.

The position of the consumer movement has been that, where competitive markets are lacking, the consumer interest can be achieved through government intervention in behalf of consumers. But in advocating this position, the consumer movement has not distinguished between "consumer sovereignty" and "consumer protection." Consumer sovereignty is control over production and the allocation of resources both in substance and by right. Consumer protection is control by government over certain elements of the economy in the name of the consumer. Because sovereignty is achieved through the market process, which coordinates individual decision-making, and protection is achieved through social intervention for specific purposes, the outcomes of the two are rarely the same. Consumer protection measures such as regulation for safe products, or even for rate or price regulation, may impose certain restrictions on producers in the name of the consumer, but they do not affirm the sovereignty of the consumer. Sovereignty, by definition, is possible only where there are competitive markets. Regulation on behalf of the consumer may bring about ad hoc changes, but it is doubtful that it can restore the competition that is the basis for the economic definition of the consumer's interest.

Related to the issue of sovereignty versus protection is that of consumer choice among alternatives, as opposed to consumer determination of what the alternatives are to be. *Sovereignty* implies not just that consumers can veto the production of some specific goods they do not want to buy, but that they have a say in what alternatives are offered. In the latter case, consumers, rather than producers, have the innovative function of what mix of goods and services is to be produced. Government regulation can do no more than prescribe limits within which business can operate; without substituting its judgment for that of consumers, regulation cannot determine what goods and services should be produced.

Showing the relationship between the consumer movement and economic theory does much to explain the ineffectiveness of the movement. This relationship is the contrast between the spirit of the consumer movement, which has sought to increase the personal well-being and satisfaction that people gain from consumption, and its doctrine, which has been tied to the rational consumer exercising independent choice in competitive markets.

The story of the consumer movement, both now and fifty years ago, is the story of its attempt to analyze consumption in terms of the rational and sovereign consumer of economic theory.

In the study that follows, Chapter 2 outlines the economic theory on which the consumer movement is based and the social and economic forces that gave the movement impetus. The rise and fall of the earlier consumer movement is dealt with in Chapter 3 which analyzes the attempts at consumer representation in the New Deal and then describes the changes World War II brought to the consumer movement and the factors that caused the movement to decline after the end of the War.

Chapter 4 traces the recent activity for the consumer in the federal government—in Congress and in the White House—and broadly outlines the various kinds of consumer protection measures that have been enacted at the state and local levels of government. The work of Ralph Nader on behalf of the consumer is taken up in Chapter 5. The role of other advocates and of consumer education is discussed in Chapter 6.

The final two chapters discuss the relation of the consumer movement to the rational consumer of microeconomic theory and explore the consequences of this theory in the further development of the movement.

2

The Theoretical Framework

[I]ndividual consumer tastes and preferences are given, . . . [and] each consumer, faced with given product prices, seeks to allocate his income among the products available in such a way that the marginal utility per dollar's worth of one will be equal to the marginal utility per dollar's worth of every other product.

Richard H. Leftwich, *The Price System and Resource Allocation*

By the end of the nineteenth century, business and agriculture, and increasingly labor, had identified and were pressing for the particular interests of their groups; but the interest of the consumer remained unarticulated. A National Consumers League has been founded in 1899 to urge people to buy goods made under fair working conditions, but this endeavor was on behalf of labor rather than the consumer.[a] At about the same time, efforts to pass a pure food and drug act (which was finally passed in 1906) focused attention on the need for direct government action to protect consumers from careless and unscrupulous manufacturers. There was also a good deal of activity in the name of the consumer during and immediately following World War I when housewives, objecting to the high prices of the period, organized groups to protest. By and large, however, until the 1920s few Americans identified themselves as consumers, and discussion of the consumer was limited to economic theory.

One exception to this must be noted. Consumer cooperatives, from their beginnings early in the nineteenth century, had been organized as a special way of meeting some of the problems consumers faced in an industrialized economy. Aside from the fact that the development of the cooperative movement in the United States has been relatively slow (compared with Europe), the concern of the cooperative for itself as a functioning entity and its members *qua* cooperators rather than *qua* consumers, has overshadowed its promotion of the consumer's role in the economy. Cooperatives have sought to handle consumer problems by going outside the mainstream of the American market structure; the consumer movement has always considered itself to be working *within* the structure.

---

[a]In recent years the League has, like organized labor, worked for the broader interests of consumers.

The Consumer in Classical Theory

Among economists, the role of the consumer has long been established. From the beginnings of classical economic analysis in Adam Smith's *The Wealth of Nations*, the consumer's wants represented the goal toward which economic activity was to be directed.

> Consumption is the sole end and purpose of all production; and the interest of the producer ought to be attended to only so far as it may be necessary for promoting that of the consumer.[1]

The consumer, in economic theory, is to come first.

But even more significant than the primacy of consumer wants, in the classical economic tradition of the nineteenth century the consumer became the "sovereign" of the economy.[2] Through their buying decisions in the market, consumers decided what goods were to be produced. Producers who turned out what consumers wanted stayed in business; those who did not were forced to accede to the consumers' wishes or go out of business. Classical theory assumed that each consumer knew what assortment of goods would go the farthest toward satisfying his particular needs and wants. In the same way, the theory assumed that the consumer knew the quality and prices of all the various goods produced and that he always chose the product having the highest quality that sold at the lowest price. Given competitive markets with many producers and many buyers, consumers were thus assured of getting the mix of goods they wanted in the highest quality and at the lowest possible price.

This view of the consumer is, of course, that of traditional laissez-faire analysis. The forces of demand on the consumer side and supply on the producer side determine the price and quantity of goods in the market. The consumer is the balancing force against the producer. Given the "invisible hand" of competition, there is no need for any outside regulation of the market. Through his demands in the market, the consumer directs the kinds of goods that are to be produced. Except for occasional imperfections in the market, stemming from limitations of time and space, there is nothing standing between the consumer and the achievement of his own best self-interest. In this analysis of the consumer's role in the economy, consumer demand is shown to be an integral factor in the determination of price; yet in nineteenth-century economics, there was little analysis of either the consumer and how his choices were made or of the process of consumption itself. Nor was there much discussion of what goods were produced, who bought them, or of changes in patterns of consumption.

The consumer and his actions did become a focal point of economic theory in the utility discussions of the nineteenth century. Through the analysis of utility, the sovereign consumer also became a rational consumer. Working on the assumption that most human beings prefer more pleasure to less pleasure and less pain to more pain the utilitarians, notably Jeremy Bentham and M. Stanley Jevons, arrived at the proposition that people want to act in such a way as to get for themselves the most pleasure and the least pain. Translating this into economic terms, it was supposed that in spending money in the market, people—consumers—would buy the goods that would provide them with the greatest pleasure, satisfaction, or utility. Like profit for the producer, utility would be the yardstick for the consumer. To achieve maximum utility, each consumer had to spend his money in such a way that the utilities from each of his final purchases were equal. Exactly how the average consumer could make these calculations was not clear, but if consumers did act in this rational way, they could know that they were getting the maximum satisfaction that their income could provide.

This highly mechanical view of consumers continued throughout succeeding revisions of the theory of consumer demand. Even Alfred Marshall in his great work, the first edition of which was published in 1890, does not say much more about consumer behavior than did the utilitarians. In his analysis, Marshall does not even explain the concept of utility, much less justify it. He assumes utility to be the measure of people's wants. Consumers compare the utility that a good will provide for them with the price of the good in the market. They will buy the good when its price is proportional to its utility. When a consumer makes a decision to buy two sets of goods, we can conclude from Marshall's analysis that the "prices [of these goods] . . . are to one another in the same ratio as their utility."[3] In spite of the fact that Marshall set out to "deal with man as he is: not with an abstract or 'economic' man; but a man of flesh and blood,"[4] we still have a consumer who rationally calculates each purchase. Marshall has to assume rationality because if consumers do not make ratios of price proportional to utility, then the usefulness of prices as a measure of wants breaks down altogether. Man is literally a *rational* consumer, and Marshall does not attempt to reconcile this view with that of the "man of flesh and blood."

Consumers' wants, first expressed in utility schedules, are translated into demand schedules; through these, consumers determine what is produced in the economy. Changes in consumer demand, by causing changes in prices, start a chain reaction through the economy until eventually equilibrium is reached. The price at which these wants can be satisfied is, of course, jointly determined by factors of both demand and supply. The analysis of consumer behavior is summed up in the demand schedule. With a consumer's choices already determined, by factors not subject to economic analysis, the only determinant of what he actually buys is price. The theory of consumption revolves about the factor of price.

Marshall was not unaware of the limitations of his analysis of consumer demand. Throughout his discussion of "Wants and Their Satisfaction," he indicated questions about consumption that he felt were important but that were outside the scope of his analysis. He pointed out that greater understanding of consumption might help to answer "the question whether our increasing wealth may not be made to go further than it does in promoting the general wellbeing."[5] In particular, he was concerned with the question of whether maximum satisfaction would actually be achieved by leaving to each person the choice to spend his income in whatever way he likes. Through the concept of consumer surplus, he showed how increases in consumer welfare could be possible by rearranging the production and consumption of certain goods. Marshall never went so far as to recommend any specific government action to achieve these ends, but he did not hesitate to suggest such a possibility.

Even though Marshall took wants as *given*, recognizing, as he noted, the traditional boundary set around English economics which excludes any discussion of wants,[6] he also recognized that the study of "wants and their satisfaction" was an integral part of "demand and consumption."[7] In his discussion of wants, he wrote of man's desire for variety and change. He suggested that man's needs are less the result of instinct than they are the result of the "development of new activities."[8] Marshall, however, put these questions aside, saying that their study belonged to the "science of efforts and activities." But he did go so far as to offer his own judgment on what kinds of wants consumers should cultivate.

If instead of seeking for a higher standard of beauty, we spend our growing resources on increasing the complexity and intricacy of our domestic goods, we gain thereby no true benefit, no lasting happiness. The world would go much better if everyone would buy fewer and simpler things, and would take trouble in selecting them for their real beauty; being careful of course to get good value in return for his outlay, but preferring to buy a few things made well by highly paid labour rather than many made badly by low paid labour.[9]

Marshall's formal structure for the analysis of the consumer in the market economy still stands in microeconomic theory. It has been refined, but not basically changed, by the later indifference curve and revealed preference analysis developed during the 1930s and afterwards. In spite of the extensive controversy and criticism surrounding these lines of thought, the consumer, in theory, still makes decisions based on given wants and preferences and determined by the relation of price to the satisfaction to be gained. In order for a consumer to be assured of maximum satisfaction from the expenditure of his income, he must have marginal utilities proportional to prices, and prices must be determined in competitive markets. In the mainstream of economic theory, the discussion of consumption and consumers has been limited to their role in determining price.

Veblen and Mitchell on Consumption

A lasting challenge to the accepted economic analysis of rational consumers maximizing utility came from Thorstein Veblen in 1899. His *Theory of the Leisure Class* provided a very different view of the American consumer. In contrast to the rational consumer of traditional theory whose dimensions of decision were for all practical purposes limited to price and utility, Veblen's analysis of the role of consumption in society opened up a broader and at the same time more tentative discussion of the place of consumption in the economy. Attention was shifted from the individual consumer's role in determining price to the consumer's personality and his relationship to the society around him. In both *The Theory of the Leisure Class* and in his more direct criticism of classical economic theory, Veblen dismissed the traditional economic theory of consumption. He abandoned the concept of utility maximization as useless for describing how consumers really behave. Veblen challenged the assumption that people as consumers are rational, acting to maximize utilities by seeking to buy goods of the highest quality at the lowest price. He argued that people seek ownership, or mere possession, of goods more than the satisfaction to be gained from their use. He substituted society for the individual as the basis for an analysis of consumption. He contrasted the facts of "growth and change" in economic life with the static assumptions of classical economics.

Veblen maintained that the primary determinant of consumption behavior is not maximization of utility but emulation of the leisure class.

It is only when taken in a sense far removed from its naive meaning that consumption of goods can be said to afford the incentive from which accumulation invariably proceeds. The motive that lies at the root of ownership is emulation.[10]

At the heart of Veblen's analysis is a society based on "invidious" comparisons between the several strata of the society. This society, according to Veblen, has always accorded high status to those who do not have to work. This leisure class is that limited number of people who for various reasons do not have to work in order to buy goods. This class indeed maintains its status through spending— Veblen's "conspicuous consumption." It is the act of spending for *ownership* rather than the means of subsistence or the satisfaction to be received from what is bought which is crucial in Veblen's analysis of consumption. Those below the leisure class in the hierarchy of society have to work, but they strive to achieve status through emulation of the spending pattern of the leisure class.

Thus people work in order to spend, not in order to buy goods that will create utilities by satisfying wants. And since it is spending that counts, "the utility of articles valued for their beauty depends closely upon the expensiveness of the articles."[11] In a reversal of economic assumptions, people shun the least-cost/best-quality criterion for a purely monetary standard of value, and because of this standard, "it results that the producers of articles of consumption direct their efforts to the production of goods that shall meet this demand for the honorific element."[12] Consumers are thus "sovereign" in that they have the power to make producers supply the kinds of goods demanded by society's pecuniary standards.

Veblen himself seemed to identify more with the "economic" consumer seeking useful goods than the consumer seeking status through conspicuous consumption, but his concepts do not prepare the way for a consumer movement. If people are guided by a pecuniary standard of worth, then any attempt to aid consumers in spending "wisely" is useless from the start.

Veblen's radical discussion provided new insight into the complex phenomenon of consumption and allowed others to break away from the traditional analysis of consumer behavior. One of these was Wesley C. Mitchell. In "The Backward Art of Spending Money" (1912),[13] he dealt with everyday problems of consumption and with the inability of people to be effective consumers. He sought to explain why people were more successful at making money than they were in spending money; why people concentrated so much more on production than on consumption.

> Important as the art of spending is, we have developed less skill in its practice than in the practice of making money. Common sense forbids our wasting dollars earned by irksome efforts; and yet we are notoriously extravagant. Ignorance of qualities, uncertainty of taste, lack of accounting, carelessness about prices—faults that would ruin a merchant—prevail in our housekeeping. Many of us scarcely know what becomes of our money.[14]

Mitchell found the explanation for this situation not in an overemphasis on people's productive role—as the consumer movement would later have it—but in the environment in which people make their spending and consuming decisions. "Our faults as spenders are not wholly due to wantonness, but largely to broad conditions over which as individuals we have slight control."[15]

What were these "broad conditions" which Mitchell said handicapped consumption? First of all, the small, simply organized family, which is the unit for spending money, stands in contrast to the large, highly organized units that business has for making money. Where a business has many workers, each with specialized and limited responsibility, the household essentially has only one person, the housewife,[16] who has sole responsibility for running the home. In the modern family, there is no specialization, little division of labor, no development of skill in purchasing. Mitchell pointed out that whole efficient businessmen are able to

> ... extend the scope of their authority, and presently be directing the work of many others: ... the limitations of family life effectually debar us from making full use of our best domestic brains. ... For the masterful housewife cannot win away the husbands of slack managers as the masterful merchant can win away the customers of the less able. What ability in spending money is developed among scattered individuals, we dam up within the walls of the single household.[17]

However capable the wife may be, she cannot hope for the same degree of success that business enterprise achieves.

In addition to the manifold responsibilities of the household manager, Mitchell pointed out that she has little in the way of technical research to draw upon. The development of sciences such as nutrition and functional psychology, which would be useful in providing for the well-being of a family, has lagged far behind the development of the sciences upon which the technology of industry depends. Nor does the family unit have any measure of costs and gain, as business does in the dollar value of costs and profit. Dollar values are not suitable for household accounting; family gains, says Mitchell, consist of "bodily and mental well-being." A family will find it very difficult to compare the costs of the gains from orthodontic work for a child, more vocational training for husband or wife, or better diet for all. Even granting some ability to make these comparisons, Mitchell pointed out that having to spend for status and effect compounds the problem of spending wisely. Housewives "must . . . make it appear that the family stands well in a world where worth is commonly interpreted as dollars' worth."[18] Finally, there is the problem of knowing for each family, and each person within the family, what are to be, in Mitchell's phrase, the "ends of living." Only in the light of a goal can a family truly measure its success in spending money.

It is hard to understand why Mitchell's description of the problems besetting the housewife has not become a classic. Had it first appeared in a magazine like *The Ladies' Home Journal* instead of in the *American Economic Review,* it might have reached a larger audience. Take, for example, this statement.

The woman must do most of her work at home, amidst the countless interruptions of the household, with its endless calls from children and friends. . . . Upon the household manager, capable or not as she may be, family life commonly throws an exhausting routine of manual labor. . . . If she has no servant, then cooking and sweeping, mending and shopping, tending the children and amusing her husband leave her little leisure and less energy for the work of management proper.[19]

Mitchell's analysis is so close to the concerns of the consumer movement that began fifteen years later that it is difficult to see why the movement has not laid greater stress on it. While the 1912 essay is often cited as an example of early interest in the problems of the consumer, there has been little discussion of it. Yet Mitchell pointed out how the size of the family unit, lack of training for household management, inability to measure costs and gains, and "conspicuous consumption" all work against successful (however that may be defined) consumption. In spite of the fact that the family is an economic unit, many of these problems do not admit to economic solutions. In particular, Mitchell's discussion of the values implicit in family spending might have given warning that education to change consumption patterns and values was on the thin edge of economics.

The Beginnings of Consumption Economics

From Mitchell's work, one can begin to trace the development of an economic analysis of consumption independent of price theory. Instead of lumping all forms of consumption together, all consumers into the rational consumer, and working from the point of view of value or price theory, this newer analysis explored the many facets of consumption: How do people spend their incomes, what determines their wants, what are consumer incomes, what is the distribution of incomes, what are the markets in which consumers buy, what is the significance of a standard of living? In contrast to demand theory which works back from the *market* to determine what consumers want, consumption theory starts with *consumers* to find out what their aims are. Consumption studies focus on consumers rather than on markets. These studies could then be explanations of consumption that are as detailed as corresponding studies of industries and the productive process.

The first such study was Hazel Kyrk's *A Theory of Consumption* published in 1923.[20] In her research, she sought to deal with the consumer's well-being in the modern, mass-production society.[21] She criticized classical economics because it passed over consumer choice. She felt that the study of consumption should be organized around standards of living, as these are the primary forces in determining what people want to consume. She pointed out that while consumer actions largely determine what is produced, consumption is equally bound by the industrial structure of the economy. Kyrk's attempt to arrive at a theory of consumption was not altogether successful because the work was essentially descriptive rather than analytical. Her discussion of the "consumer's position," however, did lead her to conclude that in a modern economy, in spite of the great gains made in total consumption, consumers lack sufficient information to make competent decisions about spending. Her concern for "independent and neutral standards" of information was exactly the concern of the consumer movement a few years later.

Kyrk's was the first in what came to be an increasing number of studies on the economics of consumption and the place of the consumer in the economy. Partly, one supposes, because of a kind of academic noblesse oblige, other disciplines have left consumer analysis to economics. Even sociology, which claims perhaps an even closer relationship to Veblen's work than does economics, has done little with consumption per se.[22] While a particular study of consumption would reflect the interest and emphasis of a particular economist, one could identify, as a "type," a group of topics, which during the 1920s and 1930s came to be included in most consumption literature. There was a concern for the aims of consumption and for the decision-making process, including the factors that influence decisions such as rational economic criteria (utility, income, and price) and cultural and social values. Material on the distribution of income and standards of living was often included. In addition, attention was given to particular areas of consumer spending—food, clothing, housing, insurance, and saving—and to the criteria that might apply to spending decisions in each of these areas. Finally, there was attention to the area of consumer protection and education by various governmental agencies at the federal, state, and local levels.

The most significant aspect of these studies was that they described a consumer who was quite different from the rational consumer of economic theory. Instead of the *he* who is the rational consumer, we see a woman, the manager of the household, who makes most of the decisions about when and how the family income is to be spent. She and her family are influenced in these decisions not only by the need for the "necessities" of life—food, shelter, and clothing—but also by the social and cultural patterns of the world around them. We see families who aspire to a standard of living which they feel appropriate for whatever group they identify with. With increasing national wealth, higher standards of living are possible, but just what new goods this higher standard ought to include for each family is not always clear. It is clear though, that the consumers attach importance to "what others think" about the goods they acquire through their purchasing decisions. These consumers are not particularly well-educated in making spending decisions and they are considerably influenced by the sellers' claims for goods. If they do have a standard of efficiency, it is quite different from the maximization standards of economic theory.

The Changing World of the Consumer

Underlying these studies of consumption was an awareness of the deeper economic and social changes that twentieth-century America brought to consumers. In the transition from an agricultural to an industrial economy, consumers were adjusting to a whole new pattern of working and spending. Instead of working for themselves, producing most of what they consumed, people worked for a wage, buying with this income most of what they consumed. Furthermore, the increasing number of working women emphasized the change from home production to ready-made goods.

With advancing industrialization and technology, more and different kinds of goods were produced and made available to consumers. The complexity and variety of these new goods put them beyond the competent judgment of most consumers as to their quality and usefulness. A housewife might know something about the differences between various kinds of "store-bought" baked goods, having her own or "mother's" home-baked as a standard, but she had no standard at all to determine the quality and value of new products with which she was totally unfamiliar such as electrical and gas appliances, new textiles and fibers, new medicines, drugs and cosmetics, and new food products. Nor were these goods limited to the pocketbooks of upper-income consumers; goods were being produced in quantities and at prices that put them within the reach of millions of American families.

But all that most consumers could know about the new goods was what the seller had to say about them—which increasingly was a great deal. As industrial technology provided the way for mass production, business found it necessary to find corresponding ways of mass selling. People needed to be made willing to buy all the new goods now available. With the development of nationwide circulation of magazines, newspapers of larger circulation, and the growing prevalence of radios in American homes, millions of consumers could be told of the new goods to be found in American markets. Through advertising and installment credit, manufacturers and distributors worked to extend the size of their markets.[b] With the proliferation of brand names on new, as well as already established, products, the consumer was faced with a bewildering variety of goods and services from which to choose.

In this world of new goods, the consumer also faced the changes brought about by being further and further removed from the seller—both from the manufacturer which now served millions of consumers and from the retail outlets which likewise served larger numbers of customers. The 1920s saw the heightened development of the large retail outlet, the chain store and the mail-order house. The personal relationship between buyer and seller that existed in small stores frequently visited by shoppers was not possible in the larger outlets. A more impersonal relationship between buyer and seller meant that the consumer had less recourse if a good were defective or did not measure up to the standards claimed for it. In such a situation, the consumer almost never had contact with a person who could be held responsible for the quality of the good he purchased.

The consumer, in addition to the adjustments made necessary by changing economic factors, was subjected as well to changing social values, which created new tensions and problems in the consumer's decisions about how to spend his income. There was the conflict between the Puritan ethic of saving and hard work and the newer gospel of spending and enjoying while one could. Consumers were torn between the traditional virtue of "living within one's means," and the increasing availability of goods through installment buying. And, finally, there was the philosophical conflict between the goal of making money in order

---

[b]The question of whether consumer credit is an abuse or contribution to consumer welfare has a long history. It can, however, be put at arm's length from the consumer movement without distorting any discussion of the history of consumer awareness. For that reason, and because it would make this study unmanageably broad, it has not been included.

to live and the goal of simply making money. These conflicts the consumer faced marked the change between a handcraft and an industrial society. As the fruits of a mass-production, industrial economy were spread throughout the nation, the conflicts touched millions of consumers.

It was not until the early 1930s that economic theory began to acknowledge the fact that modern markets did not accord to consumers the same protection and sovereignty as did the competitive markets of economic theory. Modern markets had become highly concentrated. Instead of the nameless competitors of the economic model, there were in many industries only a few firms producing a given good. Through sheer size of firms, as well as through advertising and the use of brand names, producers could remove themselves from the "reasonable" profits of the competitive model. While modern markets did not meet the conditions of a pure monopoly, they still allowed the producer a large measure of freedom to set his own price and output. In the new kind of market the best advantage of the consumer was no longer assured.

The early impetus to this new view of the American economy came largely during the 1930s from the work of Adolf A. Berle, Jr., and Gardiner C. Means in *The Modern Corporation and Private Property*[23] and from Edward H. Chamberlin's *The Theory of Monopolistic Competition.*[24] Berle and Means emphasized the extent to which the wealth of American business had become concentrated in the hands of a relatively few business concerns. In their work there was the clear implication that this new structure did not protect the consumer in the same way that the competitive structure did.

Competition between a small number of units . . . does not satisfy the [competitive] condition assumed by earlier economists, nor does it appear to be as effective a regulator of industry and of profits as they had assumed.[25]

Later, Means was more explicit in analyzing what this new form of competition meant for the consumer's interest. "The concentration [of business] into great units has steadily reduced the control which the consumer can exercise over enterprise activity through the market place."[26] With large corporations and administered prices, consumers were not necessarily assured of the lowest price consistent with the market forces of supply and demand. In addition, Means maintained that the emphasis on sales through advertising and new products further diminished the power of consumers by restricting consumer information about the comparative value of the goods they bought.

Chamberlin was more concerned with producers than with consumers, but his analysis could be used to show the extent to which the consumer was injured by the new forces within the markets. He compared the outcome of value under traditional assumptions about competition and under the new market structure. Under pure competition, the consumer was assured of the lowest price. But under anything less than perfect competition, the consumer lost not only the *assurance* but also the chance for lowest price. Given the horizontal average revenue curve of pure competition, a producer achieved his most profitable output by producing to the point where marginal cost and marginal revenue were equal. But where, through size or advertising or use of brand names, the producer was able to differentiate his product, his demand curve became, however slight, downward sloping. Under these circumstances, the equilibrium of the producer necessarily meant a higher price and lower output than would be the case under competition. In terms of traditional value theory, the consumer was not as well off as under pure competition.

The "new" economics of monopolistic competition was even less helpful to the consumer than a classical theory. The analysis of the new market structure did not say how, under the changed circumstances, the consumer's interest was to be guaranteed. Monopolistic competition, with its outcome of higher prices and lower output, showed the inadequacy of Marshall's theory of demand, but it did not provide any alternative. Ruby T. Norris was later to call Chamberlin's analysis "one revolution," and maintained that "another revolution" was needed in the analysis of consumer demand.[27] Until such a revolution, however, the consumer had no alternative but to seek either a restoration of competitive markets or governmental protection.

In spite of the fact that competition and government regulation were to be exactly the issues of the consumer movement, the impetus to the movement itself came from another direction.

3

Consumers on the March

A significant consumer movement has been born. . . . The movement is still embryonic. Yet there seems every reason to believe that the consumer movement, like the labor movement of three-quarters of a century ago, will pass from the stage of ill-coordinated and somewhat impotent groups faced with widespread distrust into a powerful agency for extending our democracy in a new direction.

Colston E. Warne, (December 1940)

The initial impetus for a consumer movement came not from the economic analysis of consumption, but from a loud and general complaint about how the American consumer was being cheated. In itself, such a complaint was nothing new—*caveat emptor* has been around for a long time. What was different was the charge that the cheating was being done on a very wide scale and included nearly all American consumers, without most of them realizing it. In *Your Money's Worth*, published in 1927, Stuart Chase and F.J. Schlink attacked what they called the "waste of the consumer's dollar."[1] They charged that through "slick salesmanship" consumers were being persuaded to buy goods at prices far above what they were actually "worth." Though one could argue the point, Chase and Schlink defined *worth* in the sense of an opportunity cost— how much it would cost if the consumer made the good himself or substituted another good that would be equally useful. They singled out products like tooth powders and mouthwash, floor cleaners, silver polish, and, especially, all sorts of patent medicines for which they said people paid prices far in excess of the cost of the "active ingredients." They maintained that through salesmanship, people were induced to buy the goods about which they knew next to nothing. "We are all Alices in a Wonderland of conflicting claims, bright promises, fancy packages, soaring words, and almost impenetrable ignorance."[2]

It was this ignorance that most concerned Chase and Schlink. Like Mitchell and Kyrk, they contrasted the extensive information based on standards and specifications that business and governments used to make their purchasing decisions with the almost complete lack of information that consumers had in their buying. They pointed out that consumers, even if they wanted to, could not make rational purchasing decisions. The extent, variety, and complexity of goods on the market made it impossible for individuals to know what would be the "best buy." Chase and Schlink maintained that it was through "the fan-fare and trumpets of higher salesmanship" that business got consumers to buy goods at inflated prices. Business was benefiting; the consumer was suffering.

As an engineer in the National Bureau of Standards, Schlink was aware of the testing services available to business and government, and what he and Chase proposed was that similar services be made available to consumers. They felt that if consumers were aware of the facts about goods, they could manage to avoid being lured by salesmanship into wasteful spending. Through wise buying, consumers would avoid wasting their own money and at the same time help to bring about more reasonable prices and more satisfactory types of goods on the market.

The Beginnings of the Consumer Movement

It was immediately evident that others shared Chase and Schlink's concern about the lack of information available to consumers. After the publication of *Your Money's Worth*, there were hundreds of letters to the authors supporting their point of view and asking for more information about specific goods. The response was so great, in fact, that Schlink realized he had the makings for the consumer information service he had been calling for. By 1929, he was able to set up Consumers' Research, Inc., which became the first testing agency in the United States devoted solely to the consumer's point of view in buying. At the start there was some help from outside, but the primary source of income to finance the staff and testing laboratory came from subscriptions to the agency's monthly publication *Consumer Bulletin*.

The wider impact of *Your Money's Worth*, however, was that it provided a focus for all the complaints about the unsettling effects of the broad economic and social changes going on around consumers. It brought the realization that the market itself, as it existed in the American economy, did not necessarily guarantee goods of the best quality at the lowest price. *Your Money's Worth* made the point that sometimes, even with a conscious effort to make wise buying decisions, the consumer, on the basis of the information available to him, was unable to do so. The sentiment began to grow that consumers, whose consumption should be the "end and purpose of all production" were at a disadvantage in the economy. Decisions about consumption actually lay, not in the hands of consumers, but in the hands of business. Production rather than consumption had become the economy's goal. Against business's power to direct production, the individual consumer had no recourse. As one commentator poignantly put it,

The consumer faces his problems alone, save for such counsel and support as other members of the family may happen to be able to give; while the produc-tive and merchandising agencies operate in increasingly coordinated masses, aided by trade associations and acute specialized services, and backed by a general governmental policy concentrated on helping business rather than the consumer.[3]

One aspect of this growing consumer sentiment was the criticism of advertising and the increasing awareness of the role that advertising played in American life. Some two years before *Your Money's Worth*, Stuart Chase had deplored the wastes in consumption associated with advertising. In categories that have a familiar ring, he argued that,

nine-tenths and more of advertising is largely competitive wrangling as to the relative merits of two undistinguished and often indistinguishable compounds— soaps, tooth powders, motor cars, tires, snappy suits, breakfast foods, patent medicines, cigarettes.[4]

For the consumer advocate, advertising came to be a symbol for the new and changing forces in the consumer's life, the new goods and new patterns of spending, the new rather than the traditional way of doing things—the power of business. Advertisers rather than consumers seemed to be directing consumption. In the words of one respected economist:

By their influence upon the valuations of millions of men, marketing experts help mold the very philosophy of the age. . . . Well may we ask whether it is wise to permit our valuations, our philosophy, our very desires to be molded by men who are guided by no higher aim than to make a profit for themselves or for their employers.[5]

Before 1929, this concern for the consumer did not have a great deal on which to build. The economy seemed to be flourishing; incomes generally were high, and consumers could choose from a greater variety of goods than ever before. Prosperity blunted discontent. Furthermore, in the prevailing economic philosophy of the time, the consumer was the arbiter of the goods produced and he should have no complaint. Under this same philosophy, it was the highly efficient American business organization that was responsible for the wonders of the growing economy and the rising standards of living for consumers. In this climate, it seemed easy to predict that the new era, when the eradication of poverty would be completed, was just around the corner.

But it was, instead, the stock market crash that was just around the corner, and the economy began to fall farther and farther from its 1929 level. In the economic climate of what was to become the Great Depression, the consumer problems that *Your Money's Worth* had brought to the attention of some became a national concern for all. As long as incomes were increasing, higher standards of living had been achieved without overconcern for how income was spent. With declining incomes and growing fear of unemployment, the problem of making ends meet loomed increasingly large for millions of consumers. More than ever, consumers could not afford any wasted dollars. Indeed, they had to make each dollar of the smaller income go farther in order to keep living standards from falling.

In the climate of economic depression, the critical attitude toward business, which was implicit in the concern for the consumer, gained new support. As the success of the American economy during the 1920s had been identified with the success of business, so the failure of the economy became the responsibility of business. The censure of business found concrete expression in the Pecora investigations into banking and the stock market and in the Temporary National Economic Committee investigations into the relationship between the high concentration of industry and the Depression. These critical examinations further enhanced the sentiment for the consumer, whose advocates had maintained all along that business had the upper hand in the economy.

Representation in the New Deal

Continuing depression was the real stimulus to a consumer movement. As the nation searched for explanations for its economic distress, more and more people identified themselves with the economic role of the consumer. As the New Deal programs for economic recovery made provision for consumer representation and as women's groups across the country took up the study of consumer problems, the outlines of a genuine consumer movement began to emerge. It was a movement of diverse groups, all of whom shared a common concern for promoting the role of the consumer in the economy.

A landmark in the emergence of a full-blown consumer movement was the attempt to provide representation for the consumer in the New Deal programs of the federal government. Under these programs, government began to participate to an unprecedented degree in economic decision-making. In this situation, a need was seen to protect the consumer's interest from being dominated by the interests of business and of labor. In one of the first of the recovery programs, the National Recovery Administration (NRA) authorized by Congress in June, 1933, the representatives of the "consuming public," along with representatives of business and labor, were to share in the formulation and administration of programs to raise national income and output. Similar programs for agriculture and, later, bituminous coal, likewise provided for the consumer to be given a voice in economic regulation. The consumer movement saw these new responsibilities as evidence that Washington had at last recognized "a private consumer problem."[6]

Because the Depression was marked by a severely declining price level that cut back profits, forced plants to close, and burdened farmers with an almost insupportable debt, the recovery programs, overall, were committed to price increases as the means for restoring economic stability. Such price increases were seen as providing profits for business and agriculture, jobs for workers, and eventually a restoration of purchasing power for the economy as a whole. In the NRA, efforts to achieve industrial recovery centered around drawing up industry "codes of fair competition." These codes were to contain provisions to shorten the work week in order to spread out jobs, and measures to raise wages in order to increase total demand. To work out these codes, consumer representatives on the Consumer Advisory Board (CAB) under the aegis of NRA, were to sit with the representatives of business and labor from each industry. It soon became clear to the CAB that the effect of the NRA industry codes would be to eliminate competition. By agreements to limit production, business could achieve its own goals of higher profits without a corresponding achievement of a higher volume of production for consumers.

This chance for consumer representation in government seemed to provide the opening wedge for national consideration of consumer problems. But the task of representation illustrated the amorphous nature of the consumer movement and its lack of clearly defined goals and programs. In the beginning, the CAB itself was not certain as to what consumer interest it represented. (By contrast, there was no doubt as to the constituencies and goals of the industry and labor representatives.) At first, the CAB asserted that it represented "the buyer of any commodity." But under pressure from the consumer movement, especially the Emergency Conference of Consumer Organizations, it finally accepted responsibility only for the *ultimate* consumer.[7] In this way, the CAB represented both the consumer bewilderment resulting from misleading advertising and lack of information about consumer goods, and the consumer's interest that, though defined in terms of competitive markets, had to be worked out in an economy of noncompetitive markets.

The amorphous nature of the consumer movement is further illustrated by the negative approach that was taken in selecting the consumer representatives. Because there was no recognized consumer body either inside or outside the government, the CAB in the NRA was appointed by the NRA administrator himself rather than by any group representing consumers, in contrast to the industry and labor advisory boards whose members were selected, respectively, by the Departments of Commerce and Labor. Furthermore, since there were few people obviously qualified to serve as advisors on behalf of consumers, it became a case of finding people with no other particular interest. And, as F.J. Schlink cynically pointed out, the CAB finally consisted of "six college professors, five club women, three government representatives, one social leader, one housewife, one cooperator and one lawyer."[8]

The greatest difficulty for consumer representation was that neither the consumer movement nor the consumer representatives had any clearly defined proposals as to what, from the consumer's view, was the best way to achieve economic recovery. They had no specific plan by which the consumer's interest in low prices and high volume and the consumer's interest in information about goods could, in a time of depression, be combined with the need to increase employment and profits. The only guide the representatives had was that, in a competitive economy, consumers were soverign and that consumption should be the "true end and purpose of all production."

As a part of its efforts to protect consumers from unwarranted price increases, the CAB tried to promote the use of standards and grades for consumer goods. These were seen as a means of counteracting higher prices by providing better consumer information about goods being sold. Such a requirement, however, would strike at the heart of modern merchandising, and, predictably, there was intense pressure brought to bear on the NRA by manufacturers and those with a stake in advertising. Without corresponding pressure in support of the consumer view, the end result was that the requirements for standards were not included in any of the codes. At the same time the persistence with which the consumer representatives pursued the matter of standards helped to lay the base for the increasing animosity of business toward the consumer view in general.

The work of the CAB was always hampered by the fact that it was never successful in convincing the NRA, particularly the administrator General Hugh S. Johnson, that there was actually a separate consumer view that required a particular set of standards to measure it. As administrator of NRA, Johnson saw his job as promoting the public interest by establishing a set of codes that would make it profitable for industry to increase production and in so doing to increase employment and the flow of goods through national markets. Johnson's position was that, as administrator, he represented the public view and that the public view and the consumer view were one. The CAB's continual criticism of the codes as inimical to the consumers' interests served only to reaffirm Johnson's position that the CAB was an unnecessary interference with the real work of the NRA.

While the CAB was arguing for the consumer interest under NRA, a parallel and equally unsuccessful process was going on in the Department of Agriculture. Under the Agricultural Adjustment Administration (AAA) passed in May, 1933, efforts were being made to raise farm incomes through restricted production and the resulting increased prices. At the beginning, at least, it was openly recognized by the AAA administrators that the effect of such a program would be contrary to the interests of consumers. The job of looking after the consumer's interests was given to a paid Consumers' Counsel set up as one of the divisions within the AAA.

The originators of the agricultural program interpreted the main task of the Counsel as that of preventing marketing channels, as distinct from agricultural channels, from using price increases to farmers as a source of increased marketing margins.[9] But the Counsel saw itself responsible as well for the larger consumer interest of maintaining low prices and high volume. It was critical of the rising prices brought by production controls; it saw the need to reform marketing channels to reduce prices to consumers. This naturally brought both producer and processor opposition. Even more, the weakness of the consumer's case against that of the producer was evidenced by the fact that "Congress had declared a clear intent in the [Agricultural Adjustment] act to have prices raised through production restriction."[10] Opposition to the Counsel was so strong that in 1935 its militantly pro-consumer staff was removed, and "there was a virtual dropping of the role of public crusader against distributors and producers on behalf of the consumer."[11]

Under the National Bituminous Coal Act of 1937, an independent Consumers' Counsel was set up "to represent the public as consumers" in the regulation of the coal industry.[12] As with industry and agriculture, the primary intent of the regulation was to raise the level of profits and wages in the coal industry by increasing the price of bituminous coal. The Counsel's position was that when government set prices, the consumer "should be assured completely of the right and opportunity to protect his interests."[13] However, little was gained for the consumer in the matter of coal prices. While mining, railroad, and other business interests had the right to argue coal prices before the National Bituminous Coal Commission, individual consumers never got the right to appear on their own behalf.

By 1940, these New Deal efforts at consumer representation were all but ended. The CAB was the first to go when the NRA was declared unconstitutional in 1935. While the Consumers' Counsel in the AAA was officially a part of the program until after the start of World War II, it maintained only a limited advisory function within the Department of Agriculture after the end of 1939. Finally, in 1939, the National Bituminous Coal Commission was replaced by the Interior Department's Bituminous Coal Division, which, along with the Consumers' Counsel, ceased to function after 1943.

The Results of Representation

These efforts at consumer representation were very nearly a complete failure. In nearly all cases regulation restricted production to achieve higher prices. The goal of higher profits and wages was put ahead of the consumer's interest in greater output at lower prices. More importantly, the consumer representatives were not able to make use of what was a unique chance to inject the consumer interest into the functioning of the economy. At no previous time had the affairs of the national economy been so open to revision; yet, as it turned out, the revision was made almost wholly according to the terms of business and labor. And when, some years later in World War II, the chance to put the consumer view into the process of economic regulation again presented itself, the inability of consumer representatives to do so stemmed from this early experience. Business and labor could ignore the consumer interest because they knew they had little to fear from this direction.

But the significance of these efforts at consumer representation is more than their apparent failure would suggest. Because these efforts represent the first deliberate attempt to incorporate the consumer's interest in government regulation and because the consumer movement looked on them as a means to further its own goals, it is helpful to a study of the movement to look at these efforts not only in terms of why they failed but also in terms of their contribution to consumer organization and to an understanding of the basic issues of the consumer movement.

There are a number of reasons for this failure to achieve genuine representation of the consumer view. The one most often cited has been the political weakness of unorganized consumers. Outside consumer pressure on government administrators and on Congress was almost totally nonexistent. Since the gain to any single consumer through a downward revision of prices would be small, there was little incentive for individual consumers to protest. By contrast, establishing higher prices meant a significant advantage to the producer or worker. Through trade associations and powerful individual businessmen, through the farm organizations and the power of the farm bloc, and through the trade unions and the labor vote, business, agriculture and labor exerted pressure for specific government regulations. This pressure was further reinforced by the Department of Commerce, Agriculture, and Labor which were established agencies supporting their respective interests. The political power of unorganized consumers was no match for the power they opposed.

Another reason for the failure of the New Deal consumer representation was the difficulty of making the consumer view generally appealing. This view called for regulations that would guarantee competition and low prices at a time when low prices and cut-throat competition had become symbols of what was wrong with the economy. In the minds of most people, the fact that "everyone is a consumer" meant that the consumer's interest was also the public interest. And the insistence of the consumer representatives on pursuing policies contrary to those generally accepted within the recovery agencies seemed to imply a disregard for the public interest. Similarly, the consumer insistence on standardized goods in an economy already deeply committed to advertising could easily be made to appear contrary to the public interest.

The consumer representatives themselves must share the responsibility for their own failure. They were novices at playing what was essentially a political game. For the most part, they were people who had not been identified with any other interest and who had come from outside the government with the idea that "consumption is the sole end and purpose of production." Their understanding of the consumer interest was in terms of the lowest price and highest quality guaranteed by competition, but they were pursuing this goal in an economy that no longer fit the competitive model. They had neither backing nor experience and could fall back only on the "rightness" of their cause.

More importantly, perhaps, consumer representation was unsuccessful because in the NRA and particularly the AAA consumer representation came to be identified with efforts to go beyond the legislative intent of the original acts to institute basic changes in the American economy.[14] Efforts to rationalize distribution, to institute grades and standards, and to provide control over advertising threatened not just the immediate goal of restricted production but the established patterns of business operation as well. These efforts implied that the consumer interest could not be fulfilled except by sacrifices on the part of producers—gains for consumers would mean losses for producers. In the economic and political crosscurrents of the thirties, many identified the consumer interest with radical and somehow un-American change.

But while the consumer representatives did not succeed in injecting the consumer interest into the process of government regulation of the economy, they did contribute toward an understanding of the basic issues of the consumer movement. They began to articulate the limits of the consumer's interest in a changing economy where the forces of the market could not longer be relied on to protect the consumer interest. Where there was to be government regulation of areas of the economy, they recognized the need for consumer advocacy to balance the influence of other special interests. And, finally, their inability to generate this support led them to the conclusion that the inherent weakness of consumers meant, inevitably, the need for government support to right the balance. In a final memorandum before its dissolution in 1935, the members of the CAB stated the need for permanent consumer representation.

Such an agency might take the form of a Department of the Consumer or of a Consumers' Commission. This agency would tie together the work of separate government bureaus affecting the consumer and would act as spokesman between the consumer and the Government. It would collect and distribute information of value to the consumer. It would promote the establishment of standards, grades and labelling for consumers' goods.[15]

In spite of the failures of consumer representation, the consumer movement was growing. Consumers' Research was joined in 1936 by another testing organization, Consumers Union.[a] Several attempts were made to start a large, central consumer organization at the national level to bring together a number of local consumer organizations that were scattered across the country. Women's organizations like the American Association of University Women and the National League of Women Voters adopted the promotion of the consumer view as part of their overall programs. Consumer education in school and in

---

[a]Consumers Union was started by some dissident members of Consumers' Research who left following a dispute over establishing a labor union within Consumers' Research. As head of Consumers' Research, Schlink maintained that his organization was directed solely toward serving the consumer and refused to associate it with any other cause.

adult life came to be viewed as a means to help people become wise consumers and to create an effective consumer constituency. Consumer pressure aroused by the so-called "guinea pig"[16] books is generally credited with the passage of the 1938 food and drug law, even though the law as finally passed was so limited in scope that Schlink called it worse than nothing. (However limited it might have been, this measure turned out to be the only lasting accomplishment of the 1930's movement.)

But the most significant evidence of the growth of the consumer movement was the growing awareness of it on the part of the business community. Increasingly, in all the consumer activity—the interest of women's groups, the "guinea pig" books, agitation for the pure food and drug law, news and publicity about the consumer—business saw an antibusiness bias. It saw the growing consumer movement as a direct threat to its own interests.

The point of greatest friction between business and the consumer movement was advertising. From the beginning, the consumer movement had attacked excessive and misleading advertising, and as the years went by, this criticism grew stronger. The movement resented the power of advertising over consumer values and asserted that advertising was a major force in establishing the patterns of American consumption. It saw advertising as often encouraging people to use their incomes in unwise and essentially wasteful expenditures. The consumer movement maintained that there was considerable evidence to the effect that highly advertised goods were nearly always higher in price and just as often of lower quality than similar unadvertised products. It was particularly critical of advertising that emphasized the emotional rather than the intelligent reasons for buying a good—such as buying to achieve popularity, success, or status. According to the consumer movement, advertising, instead of providing information that would assist consumers in making wise buying decisions, succeeded only in adding to their confusion—and vulnerability.

This criticism of advertising was an affront to all of business. Business did not argue that advertising was not a potent force in consumer decisions to buy. Its first line of defense was to assert that, through advertising, business had been able to create mass markets and thus to increase the availability of goods. This meant, advocates claimed, more goods at lower prices for consumers. Just as important, business held that advertising was necessary to economic stability and that it operated to maintain the flow of demand for industry's output of goods.

In addition, business defended advertising as a positive contribution to consumers that made them aware of the wide variety of goods available to them. It provided people with choices, giving the individual the opportunity to spend his money as he liked. Thus, by implication, to distrust advertising was to oppose choice. Since choice is inherent in American democracy, to distrust advertising was to be un-American. Business also argued that "wise buying," in the sense of highest quality for lowest price, is not necessarily that which gives the consumer the greatest satisfaction. There was the further psychic satisfaction that could come from buying highly advertised goods. As a further argument, business held that people did not take the superlatives in advertising literally anyway. It accused the consumer movement of blanket criticism of advertising and of failure to emphasize the great contribution that advertising made to the modern American economy.

Business met the challenge of the consumer movement in a variety of ways. In some instances, it sought to discredit it. It was viewed either as falsely representing the interests of the consumers or as a force outside the tradition of the American economy. On the old assumption that "if you can't lick 'em, join 'em," there were also efforts on the part of business to set up their own consumer organizations. These sought to pose their own aims as those of the consumer movement. Other business elements sought to provide a common ground for discussion of consumer and producer problems; as a result, the National-Consumer-Retailer Council was set up to discuss labeling and standards. The Council was composed of business people and representatives from the women's groups in the consumer movement. The National Better Business Bureau had worked for a number of years to promote "high standards of business enterprise" and took on the job of cooperating with the consumer movement as part of their special competence. Many local branches of the Better Business Bureau set up consumer advisory panels to work on problems in particular areas.

By the end of the thirties, even business began to concede that the consumer movement was a new, and growing, force in the American economy and one with which it would have to deal. *Business Week* formally acknowledged the consumer movement in its issue of April 22, 1939, in a "Report to Executives" tracing the origin and development of the consumer movement which, according to the writer, had "spread like wildfire" and was growing "in force and vigor."

The Consumer Movement in the Wartime Economy

The increase in government activity brought on by the beginning of the war in Europe in late 1939 raised for a second time the hopes of consumer groups for effective representation of the consumer in the making of national economic policy. The chance came in 1940 when the National Defense Advisory Commission set up the Consumer Division headed by a consumer commissioner with broad responsibility for consumer interests and consumer protection in the governmental planning for a wartime economy. With an eagerness reminiscent of the consumer representatives in the earlier New Deal agencies, the Consumer Division set to work. It saw itself as responsible for protecting, as far as possible in a national emergency, all aspects of consumer welfare—income, nutrition, housing, and morale. It felt that consumption efficiency would enable consumers to make a positive contribution to the war effort.

As defense preparations progressed during late 1940 and early 1941, consumer leaders became concerned about increasing prices and the growing shortage of consumer goods. They felt that the government should take action to relieve the pressure on prices. If business were pushed to expand output, consumers could be provided with goods at relatively stable prices. But the Consumer Commissioner's power in these matters was slight. There had been no Presidential directive "to give weight and guidance" to the Consumer Division, and in the press or wartime events advocacy of the consumer's interest claimed national attention only occasionally. Without a public pressure group, the commissioner could do little more than plead for the consumer at conferences and in after-dinner speeches. Within a year after the Division was set up, a consumer leader could speak bitterly of the Consumer Division, "hidden away in a Washington back alley; . . . inadequately staffed, and . . . not given the power to meet the national consumer crisis."[17]

In 1943, in the House of Representatives, an informal committee of about fifteen members was organized "to protect the consumer," but after this expression of interest, little additional work was done. In that same year, the Office of Price Administration (OPA) set up the Consumer Advisory Council to parallel similar industry and labor committees. The members of the Council were chosen from national organizations expressing a consumer interest and from "leaders in the fields of consumer economics, marketing, clothing, food and public relations."[18] The Council was strictly advisory and seems never to have carried much weight.

In a very real sense, however, the OPA in its responsibility for rationing and price control was a consumer agency, and consumer leaders felt that consumer-oriented measures like grade labeling continued to be subordinated to business pressure. To maintain effective price control, the OPA undertook to set standards of quality. In this way, producers would be denied price increases that were achieved through quality degradation. The OPA had been using standard grades on a few goods—meat, dairy products and women's rayon hosiery—without much opposition. But when in 1943, OPA announced that all fruits and vegetables would have to be canned under grade standards, it brought upon itself a deluge of criticism from manufacturers and business in general.[19] As a result, by language included in an appropriations bill passed by Congress, the OPA was explicitly forbidden to require of manufacturers any sort of grade specification.

The real impact of the war on the consumer movement was not so much that the consumer's interest was often overridden but that the consumer movement subordinated its own goals to those of the consumer at war. Consumer advocates unhesitatingly promoted the "consumer in defense" and later "the consumer in wartime." Through consumer education, the Consumer Division, and the broad base of support in the women's organizations, consumer advocates turned the work of consumers toward the war effort. Consumers were urged to buy wisely, to serve nutritious meals, to accept rationing and price control. Being a "good" or "conscientious" consumer came to represent the contribution that the "home front" could make toward the total war effort. In the end the effect of the war was to interrupt the growth and obscure the goals of the consumer movement.

The ten years after the end of World War II saw the continued decline of the consumer movement. In the first place its goals were out of tune with the postwar national mood. The consumer movement had required of its constituents a sober, rational, almost austere, attitude toward the economy. The consumer was required to think before he acted and to consider carefully in the light of his basic goals all the alternative purchases open to him. He had to sort out from the barrage of advertising and other sales techniques what was information and what was sales pressure. Such sobriety appeared seemly during the uncertain years of the Depression and in wartime. But the end of the war broke the restraints. For the first time since before the Depression, there were both goods to buy and money to buy them with. No longer could the "war effort" demand that people hold off spending; incomes were higher than they had ever been and there was little unemployment. For many people, there was a backlog of savings greater than they had ever known. People started buying whatever was available with a thorough disregard for the tenets of prudent consumership.

There was also the nearly universally held view that the end of the war brought an end to the need for government regulation. Both the Depression and war had brought a degree of government regulation, especially of business, previously unknown in the United States. With peace and a flourishing economy, there seemed to be no need for continuing government direction of the economy. And where business had been on the defensive during the thirties, business and industry now received much of the credit for winning the war. Business became interested in selling itself as a responsible agent in American economic life, able to operate effectively and profitably only while serving its customers to their own best advantage.[20] In this atmosphere it was difficult to exploit the antagonism between consumer and producer that had nourished the earlier efforts of the consumer movement.

Finally, the shift in economic thinking from classical microeconomic theory to Keynesian macroeconomic theory had the effect of de-emphasizing the individual consumer of the consumer movement. As long as academic economics focused on the marketplace and the price resulting from interaction between seller and buyer, the consumer movement could identify its concerns with those of current economic discussion. But in macroeconomic theory the buying decisions of the individual consumer were of less interest than the total amount of spending of all consumers.[21] The power of the consumer was no longer in terms of how his decision to buy or not to buy affected a single producer; rather it was the power of all consumers, who by buying or not buying, helped to determine the level of employment in the economy as a whole. In economic theory, the consumer in the marketplace, choosing between different types of goods, changed to consumers in the economy, deciding to increase or decrease the proportion of income that they spent rather than saved.

This shift in the focus of economic theory isolated the concerns of the consumer movement for the "sovereign consumer." "Consumption" and "household behavior" became macroeconomic variables. With attention centered on total spending and the level of employment, the emphasis of economic theory was again on production. The significance of consumer spending was in its effect on the level of production and output, rather than in its contribution to consumer satisfaction. In spite of the fact that after World War II the *consumer* became more than ever the object of research, the macroeconomic view of the consumer was not in accord with that of the consumer movement.

The postwar weakness of the consumer movement is evidenced by its lack of response to circumstances which in the 1930s would have provided a new spur for consumer activity. In the three years following the end of the war, the Consumer Price Index rose nearly twenty points. There were some scattered buyers' strikes around the country, particularly in the New York area. There was also another attempt, in 1947, to establish a national association of consumers, but in spite of an illustrious group of sponsors, the organization was no more successful than its predecessors had been.[22] Nor was there an effective consumer movement to call for representation of its view in government when, with the outbreak of the Korean war, the nation again faced the prospect of economic regulation. In the hearings on the Defense Production Act of 1950, the only evidence that could be said to have been presented on the consumer's behalf were letters from the Consumer Conference of Greater Cincinnati, the American Veterans Committee, the Central Labor Union of Charleston, South Carolina, and the South Carolina Federation of Post Office Clerks.

A Revival in the Fifties

Given the decline of the consumer movement during and after World War II, it is difficult to isolate direct causes for the revival of interest in the consumer that began in the 1950s and that has been growing ever since. A number of events can be said to contribute to it. Two widely read books, *American Capitalism* by John Kenneth Galbraith and *The Hidden Persuaders* by Vance Packard, raised issues that were highly relevant to the individual consumer. The monopoly hearings begun in 1957 under Senator Estes Kefauver were the first in a series of Congressional hearings that focused attention on the consumer. And, finally, consumer protection became headline news in the cranberry and thalidomide cases.

Galbraith's *American Capitalism*, which appeared in 1952, emphasized the market or microeconomic aspects of the American economy and gave consumer advocates new ammunition in their fight for the consumer interest. Galbraith pointed out that even though competition in the classical economic sense no longer prevailed in the American economy, the expected results of such competition—a high volume of goods at reasonable prices—did prevail. To explain this phenomenon, Galbraith propounded the concept of "countervailing power." According to Galbraith's argument, power on one side of the market brought into being a countervailing power on the other side of the market. Thus industrial power on the part of large manufacturers brought into being labor unions on the one hand and large retail distribution units on the other. The cross-effects of these large aggregates of economic power brought about the results, if not the mechanism, of classical competition.

While Galbraith did not make the point, those groups concerned with the consumer position used his arguments to make a case for the need for a stronger presentation of the consumer's view. By shifting the emphasis of the theory of countervailing power and stressing the notion of a balance, consumer advocates could use Galbraith's theory to support the need for consumer power through organization. They could further argue that Galbraith's analysis justified government support to consumers in the same way that government support had been provided to agriculture and labor under the New Deal. (Consumers could also recall their failure to realize effective government support during that same period.) If an economic group were too weak to have effective countervailing power in its own behalf, it would be necessary for government to provide it.

In a very different way, the consumer's position in the economy was at issue five years later in Packard's *The Hidden Persuaders* (1957). Lashing out at the use of techniques made possible through motivation research, Packard pictured the American consumer as being manipulated by business to its own end. Packard maintained that through motivation research, business led people to buying decisions through subconscious rather than rational processes. Through advertising that played upon their unspoken, often unrealized, wants and emotions, consumers were unknowingly made the pawns of business. According to Packard, the problem was not that people were always induced to buy the "wrong" good; the problem was the power over consumers that business had acquired through its marketing techniques. Whether for "good" or "bad" purposes, Packard accused business of manipulating consumers to its *own* purpose.

The Hidden Persuaders was not unlike *Your Money's Worth*. Both were "exposés" of what business would, and could, do to the consumer to make him buy goods. The implication of both books is that because business has the upper hand in the marketplace, the consumer is not the master of his own decisions. Packard did not make his case in the name of the consumer, but there was much in his thesis that echoed Schlink and the earlier consumer movement.

The Congressional hearings on monopoly power and administered prices, which were begun in 1957,[23] led Senator Estes Kefauver to hold essentially the same position the consumer movement had maintained for twenty-five years. Kefauver saw in concentrated industries the same restricted output and higher prices that the consumer movement had criticized in the recovery programs. He concluded that in an economy where large industrial units had considerable market power, the position of the consumer was so weak that it justified the support of the federal government. To this end, Kefauver proposed not only that a Department of the Consumer be established, but that the consumer interest also be protected through more stringent regulation of the economy to assure genuine competition. He maintained that antitrust policy was not effective to curb the growth of monopoly power and that regulatory agencies, more often than not, were more concerned with regulating competition among firms within an industry than with regulating industry in the public interest. As a long-range solution to consumer problems, Kefauver called for the reinstatement of competitive conditions in the American economy and a government policy that combined effective regulation with "the spotlight of publicity" on monopoly.

Finally, consumer protection got extensive publicity from two incidents involving the Food and Drug Administration (FDA). Just before Thanksgiving, 1959, the FDA ordered large quantities of cranberries off the market because they had been sprayed with chemicals which in laboratory tests caused cancer in rats. (No conclusive evidence was available on the effect of the chemical on human beings.) As a result, sales for all cranberries at what would normally be the peak season fell off drastically. The cranberry growers protested what they thought was an abuse of government power.[24] The press generally maintained that since there was no proven connection between the chemical and cancer in human beings, the FDA had acted precipitously. On the other side, consumer advocates backed the FDA and its efforts to enforce pure food laws.[25]

In early 1962, it became known that thalidomide, a new tranquilizing drug that was being distributed to physicians on a clinical basis by its manufacturer, was strongly linked with birth defects.[26] The public press carried many pictures and accounts of the affected children. Even though the FDA had power to forbid outright marketing of thalidomide in the United States (and indeed was exercising that power), the thalidomide case became associated in the public mind with the need for stronger government regulation of drugs and became the basis of support for a bill originally sponsored by Kefauver to control monopoly in the drug industry. As finally passed, the measure considerably extended the control of the FDA over licensing of new drugs, but less was done to protect the economic position of the consumer with regard to drugs.

Thus the groundswell of a renewed interest in the consumer had begun. The consumer was news again.

Governments and the Consumer

Consumer protection fosters a marketplace in which our competitive economic system flourishes best.

Richard M. Nixon (February 1971)

The governmental advocacy that began with Kefauver has continued and expanded. In contrast to the earlier period, consumer issues have come to have considerable political appeal. Congress has passed dozens of consumer bills and has come close to enacting legislation that would provide for a permanent consumer agency in the federal government. Presidents now appoint consumer advisors and send special messages to Congress detailing consumer needs. All fifty states have designated some sort of agency to be responsible for consumer protection, and since 1960 thirty-nine states have passed various consumer protection statutes.[1] In contrast to the thirties when the consumer movement was almost entirely outside government, now more often than not government takes the lead, with nongovernmental consumer organizations responding to its initiative.

But if there has been a shift in the locus of consumer activity, there has not been any change in its direction. As before, attention is still focused on the consumer and his position in the marketplace. Governmental support for the consumer continues to define the consumer's interest in terms of competition and information. Just as a consumer spokesman in 1938 said that consumers were working for "income, information, integrity, and independence,"[2] so today the President's Committee on Consumer Interests lists the consumer's right to "safety, information, choice, and a hearing." Advocates still maintain that the necessary competition and information to assure these rights are lacking and that government must therefore intervene in the consumer's behalf.

The Initiative in Congress

Consumer legislation in Congress can be divided roughly into three categories. The first category includes legislation like truth in packaging or lending which seeks to protect the consumer's pocketbook. The second category includes measures like the food and drug act, cigarette labeling and advertising act, and the establishment of the Consumer Product Safety Commission that deal with consumer health and safety. Finally, in the third category are measures to enhance the power of consumers in the political decision-making process.

The truth in lending and the truth in packaging measures passed in 1968 and 1966, respectively, are particularly relevant to a study of the consumer movement. Not only were they a kind of "breakthrough"[3] in consumer legislation, but they also focus on the same question with which the movement began in 1927—the consumer's information about the goods he buys. In the hearings on both bills, the issue turned on whether the consumer had the kind of information necessary for genuine bargaining between consumer and seller. The passage of these bills served notice that Congress was willing to intervene in the economic process between consumer and producer.

The truth in lending bill was first introduced in 1960. The bill's basic provision was that, in all credit transactions, lenders should state credit charges in terms of a simple annual interest rate. Hearings were held in 1960, 1962, 1963, and 1967. In all the hearings, the testimony for and against the measure was remarkably consistent from one year to the next. The basic issues were whether consumers wanted and needed to know how much interest they were paying for credit and whether lenders should be burdened with the duty of calculating and disclosing such charges. Consumer advocates testifying for the measure based their argument on the need for consumers to have adequate information if the market system were to function efficiently. They argued that the confusing complexity of credit charges was such that consumers had no way of comparing the costs of credit. Opposition to the measure came primarily from lending institutions which saw the measures as an implied criticism of the prevailing rates of installment credit and an attempt at government control of credit institutions.

It is worth noting that both advocates and opponents of the bill were talking about a consumer who had come to see buying on credit as a reasonable and sure way of acquiring goods without having to wait and save to buy them. For millions of American families, credit had become a "way of life" not only for the purchase of homes and cars but also for a myriad smaller durable and not so durable goods. In the 1960 hearings, George Katona noted that, for example, "a person who chooses to buy on the installment plan is commonly characterized as intelligent, as informed, as one who plans ahead, or as cautious and conservative."[4] A strong bill was finally passed in 1968. It included not only provisions for credit disclosure to foster the "informed use of credit" but also provisions to limit the amount of a worker's wage that can be garnished and to set criminal penalties against loan sharks.

In 1961, within a year after the introduction of the first truth in lending bill, Senator Phillip A. Hart began hearings on what came to be called the "Truth in Packaging" legislation.[5] The genesis of the packaging hearings was not unlike that of the original consumer movement—the proliferation and continually changing array of new consumer goods. Goods on the shelves were available in a wide variety of brand names, packages, and sizes; competition between products had come to be based as much on advertising and packaging as on prices. Consumers, it was said, had to decide among some eight thousand different items in a typical large supermarket. During the hearings, the "eight thousand different items" was used repeatedly by both sides. Consumer spokesmen used it to show the difficulty the consumer faced in trying to make rational choices among such a large variety of goods. Business used it to show the great strides that industry had made in providing an increasing array of goods from which consumers could choose. The positions taken in the hearings are interesting because they do much to illuminate the basic conflict between business and consumer advocacy.

Consumer advocates maintained that the determination of a "best buy" was made difficult by a bewildering and changing assortment of package sizes and designs, fractionalized weights, designations like "large economy size" and "jumbo quarts" and "slack-filled" packages. They maintained that rational decision-making by consumers was an essential part of the efficient operation of the American market system. They held that business practices were subverting the system by discouraging consumers from making rational purchasing decisions. Consumer advocates also implied that business often knowingly presented weight and price information and designed packages to confuse consumers. What was needed, they said, was legislation that would set standards for packaging and labeling.

Opponents of the bill held that such legislation was an unnecessary interference by government into matters that were the prerogative of private business. They maintained that goods presently carried all the price and weight information required for "best buy" determination. The hearings included lengthy discussion of whether the American housewife-consumer was, or was not, able, with or without a slide rule, to compute per-unit costs. One food industry representative asserted that "the housewife . . . should be expected to take the time to divide fractionalized weight into fractionalized prices."[6] Business witnesses further maintained that the authority needed to control dishonest practices was already held by the regulatory agencies and that other consumer complaints were unwarranted. They asserted that, because of the efforts of American business to provide new and different goods, present day American consumers were better off than any others in the world. Regulation would not only curb business efforts to provide new goods for consumers it would also interfere with the consumer's basic right to choose. One industry representative went so far as to assert that "to outlaw packaging with its design and color is to outlaw our way of life."[7]

In spite of persistent producer efforts to defeat the measure, legislation was finally passed in 1966. *Consumer Reports* said the law fell "short of what it should be " but declared it "something of a legislative miracle" that any version was passed.[8] The bill provided the basis for FDA, Federal Trade Commission

(FTC), and the Secretary of Commerce to require manufacturers to print quantity and price statements on packages in such a way as to facilitate these "value comparisons." Industry was given a year to work out its own "voluntary" standards of packaging sizes, after which the FDA and FTC were given "discretionary" authority to begin to set up obligatory standards. The FDA also was given discretionary authority over the use of terms such as "family size," "jumbo," and the use of "cents off" as a promotion technique. Regulations were authorized, but not required, to present "slack-fill" packages.

There has been little long-range effect of the "legislative miracle." After its passage, toothpaste manufacturers voluntarily reduced the number of package sizes to five, but ten years later there were more than a dozen different sizes, all in fractional weights.[9] The same situation exists for countless other consumer products. Much more has been gained for consumer "value comparisons" by the unit pricing recently instituted by many large supermarkets than has been accomplished by the truth in packaging legislation.

In contrast to the strenuous opposition and long debates generated by the lending and packaging bills, consumer health and safety measures have proved to be less antagonistic to Congress. During the past twenty years, a number of such laws have been enacted, including measures pertaining to auto safety, flammable fabrics, pesticides, radiation, harmful toys, gas pipelines, and cigarette labeling.

Health and safety legislation is as unpalatable to the affected industry as is legislation passed to protect the consumer's pocketbook. Congress, however, has more readily accepted measures designed to protect consumers' physical well-being. Part of the explanation for this is that when a measure focuses on the economic status of the consumer, there is an implied interference with the free market; opposition to the measure can always be relatively safely couched in terms of the market mechanism and free consumer choice. But the free market argument is not so compelling in the case of people's health and safety. Furthermore, consumers themselves respond to dangers of disease and accident through the press and in letters of Congress. Kefauver's 1962 drug bill was passed primarily because of the national scare over the distribution of dangerous drugs; similar circumstances have eased the passage of other such measures.

In 1972, in response to this continuing concern for health and safety, Congress passed legislation establishing the Consumer Product Safety Commission. The Commission, which some say is "probably the most powerful regulatory agency ever created by the government,"[10] is charged with protecting consumers from harmful or hazardous goods among the thousands of products bought and used by consumers with the exception of automobiles. It has the power to set standards for safety, to ban from sale or to recall products, and to make surveys on types of hazardous products. (In an unusual procedure, the legislation has provided consumers with the right to participate in the drafting of safety standards.) The Commission also has power to institute criminal proceedings against companies which do not obey its orders. The Commission which has a staff of more than 800 has not yet set any mandatory safety standards, but it has recalled products, banned others from sale, and identified some five million items with "substantial product hazards."[11]

While these consumer protection measures represent restrictions on large and powerful industries, it has also been suggested that the bills finally passed by Congress represent victories for producers as often as for consumers. In spite of the mounting evidence relating cigarettes and cancer, the Cigarette Act of 1965, for example, only required a mild warning on each package and carton but postponed the requirement for any such warning in advertising until 1969. An amendment to the Cigarette Act in 1970 prohibited radio and television advertising of cigarettes but to date, legislation to bar all types of cigarette advertising has not been successful. Nor has the power conferred on the Product Safety Commission been widely used. The Commission has been without a full-time director during much of its existence. Consumers complain that the Commission has been slow to act and "feeble and ineffective" in its compliance work.[12]

The effort to enhance the power of the consumer in the political decision-making process has long been an issue before Congress. From their experience in the New Deal, consumer advocates in 1935 called for a "Department of Consumers" which would provide for consumers the kind of bargaining strength given by the Departments of Commerce, Labor, and Agriculture to their constituents. Some thirty years later, Kefauver unsuccessfully sponsored legislation for an independent consumer agency in the executive branch of the government after twice seeing his bills to establish a separate consumer department defeated. In 1966, hearings on another proposal for a Department of Consumers were held, but no action was taken. Beginning in 1969, bills have been introduced and hearings held on the establishment of a federal consumer agency in every session of Congress. The increasing support for such an agency suggests that its realization is only a matter of time.

In general, there have been three approaches to setting up an agency that would represent the consumers' interest in Washington: a cabinet-level department, an independent federal agency, and a statutory office in the executive office of the President. The legislation first suggested by Senator Kefauver in 1963 and later sponsored by Representative Rosenthal in the House called for a cabinet-level department. Such a consumer department would consolidate the responsibilities for consumers—responsibilities that are now scattered throughout the federal government. It would both represent and coordinate consumer interests throughout the federal government. Partly because of lower cost (cabinet budgets are several times those of agency budgets), and partly because of lower visibility and power, the first kind of consumer representation to receive approval by either house was a separate federal agency. The Senate bill passed in 1970 authorized an independent agency with emphasis on advocacy of consumer interests before the federal regulatory agencies of cabinet-level departments. The third form of consumer representation that has often been proposed is a Congressionally established office of consumers in the executive office of the President. This last seems to have been favored as "the best of a bad lot" by business interests anxious to minimize the ability of consumers to intervene in regulatory affairs and by members of Congress anxious to avoid enlarging the federal bureaucracy.

In the last days of the 91st Congress, the Senate passed the Consumer Protection Organization Act, but a similar measure failed in the House of Representatives. In 1971, the House passed a consumer agency bill, but no action was taken on the measure in the Senate. In 1972 and again in 1974, a bill to set up a consumer-protection agency was passed in the House but was defeated both times by a filibuster in the Senate. Early in 1975, the Senate passed a bill setting up an "Agency for Consumer Advocacy." In November, the House passed an amended version of the Senate bill. President Ford has argued against such an agency and has suggested he will veto it. The question is whether or not Congress will be able to override the veto.

The measures, which since 1970 have variously received House or Senate approval, would create an independent agency which most often has been referred to as a Consumer Protection Agency or CPA. (Recently, certified public accountants have objected to CPA and have suggested instead an "Agency for Consumer Protection," or ACP.) The primary responsibility of such an agency would be to represent and advocate consumer interests before federal regulatory agencies. It would also receive consumer complaints and be able to call on businesses for answers to specific questions. Proponents of the legislation point out that "the terms of economic transactions are set not in the marketplace . . . but in the governmental agencies through a political bargaining process,"[13] and cite the close relationship between the regulatory agencies and the regulated industries as evidence of this process. They maintain that in this close relationship the consumer more often than not is the loser and that an agency is needed to represent the consumer's interest which is that which would be obtained "in a free market economy characterized by vigorous competition, economic efficiency, and optimal consumer information."[14]

Opponents of the CPA base their case on the proposition that there are already too many agencies in the federal government and that a consumer agency only further enlarges the federal bureaucracy with accompanying increases in expense and red tape. They also argue that there is a "vague" grant to intervene and no precisely defined "consumer interest." They maintain that without an identifiable consumer interest, the decision as to what that interest is will rest wholly with the agency, which, it is often said, will be controlled by consumerists out to harass legitimate business. Opponents also argue that the way to protect consumer interests is not to set up another agency but to strengthen already existing ones. In particular, business opposes any legislation that would provide the CPA with the authority to open company books.

In spite of the sameness of the arguments pro and con from year to year, there have been some changes in the identity of the spokesmen. Most notable is the fact that long-time supporters such as the consumer organizations and the AFL-CIO have been joined by a few large firms such as Montgomery Ward, Polaroid, and Mobil Oil. On the other hand, the National Association of Manufacturers, the Chamber of Commerce, and Grocery Manufacturers of America continue to stand opposed.

The bill passed in 1975 was not as strong as consumer proponents wished. The CPA would have power to intervene in the formal proceedings of federal regulation but could participate in informal proceedings only at the regulatory agency's discretion. The CPA would not itself have subpoena power but could request other agencies to use theirs on its behalf. It could, however, ask the federal courts to review any regulatory decisions which it felt were adverse to the consumer's interests. In spite of these shortcomings, it is certainly true that the consumer advocates would hail the establishment of a CPA as a milestone in the history of the consumer movement.

The prospect of the establishment of a consumer agency in the federal government, and with it the "transition" from safety to economic issues,[15] raises the question of what has happened to create in Congress this supportive atmosphere for consumer affairs. The consumer issues on which Congress has acted in the seventies are little different from those of twenty or even forty years ago. What has brought such political support to "the consumer's interest"?

The answer may have less to do with a worsening state of consumer affairs than with other changes at work in American society. In an era in which there has come to be increasing distrust of both business and government, sympathy for the consumer seems to put legislators on the side of people against the powerful and impersonal forces which big business and big government appear to embody.

There are, first of all, political reasons for increased Congressional interest in consumer legislation. The persistently high level of inflation since 1970 has brought Congressional attention to the consumer's situation. With opinion polls continuing to show inflation as a primary public concern, sympathy for consumer issues, even those not directly related to inflation, would be seen by legislators as a way to gain consumer support. In fact, legislative action on issues like consumer representation in government can even be a substitute for inaction—and uncertainty as to how to act—on inflation. The fact that consumer legislation does not require large appropriations also makes it attractive to legislators and voters.

This Congressional concern for the consumer is reinforced by the continuing economic debate about the size of American business units—in industry and finance, as well as in agriculture. In this debate the focus is on the consumer. This is true whether from the point of view of the Galbraithians who argue that size is technologically based and requires some form of government supervision of prices, or from the point of view of those in the Friedman camp who affirm the efficiency of competition, even among a relatively small number of firms, to bring about lower prices and reasonable levels of profits. The focus of debate is also on the consumer in the growing discussion of the need to deregulate large segments of American industry. The argument here is that federal regulatory agencies such as the Interstate Commerce Commission, the Federal Communications Commission, and the Civil Aeronautics Board have become captives of the industries which they were created to regulate, and that deregulation of air, rail, and truck transportation, for instance, would free up competitive forces to provide consumers with better service at a lower cost.

Finally, the disarray of American politics makes the *consumer* politically more appealing than the *voter*. Voters appear to bear a responsibility for the widely acclaimed "loss of integrity" in government. But consumers are seen as individuals and households, unsullied by governmental malfeasance. (This is also Ralph Nader's theme, a point to be discussed in the following chapter.) Political support for consumers is seen as reaffirming the personal and even moral values in an increasingly impersonal and immoral society.

Presidential Support for the Consumer

The first president to give his specific support and sympathy to the consumer's cause was John F. Kennedy. On a number of occasions during the 1960 Presidential campaign, Kennedy identified the voter as a *consumer* and promised that if he were elected he would create the office of a consumer counsel to assure that the consumer's interest would be heard in Congress and in the proceedings of government regulatory agencies. In 1962 in what was the first special message to Congress on the consumer, Kennedy identified what he called the consumer's "bill of rights." Consumers, Kennedy claimed, should have the right to safety, the right to be informed, the right to choose, and the right to be heard. To protect these "rights," Kennedy called for increased activity and appropriations for the regulatory agencies which acted on the consumer's behalf, mentioning specifically the ICC, CAB, FTC, and FCC. As an assurance of government attention to consumer matters, the head of each federal agency particularly concerned with consumer affairs was to appoint a special assistant for consumer affairs within the agency to "advise and assist" within the agency and "to act as liaison" between the agency and consumer organizations. Little notice was given to the fact that these assistants were thus consumer representatives in agencies already charged with a consumer responsibility. In all, twenty-two such assistants were appointed, ten from departments and twelve from federal agencies.

Kennedy's promised consumer counsel turned out to be an advisory council of consumers in the Council of Economic Advisors. Consumer advocates saw the CEA's Consumer Advisory Council as the first real opportunity for true consumer representation in government. They hailed it as a "remedial action" for a long-felt need.[16] But the Council was little more than window-dressing, and, even by its own accounting, it could find no instance where it was able to improve the consumer's status. In its *First* (and only) *Report*, the Council recorded that it "issued statements" favoring the lending and packaging bills, "took a position" favoring tax revision; "endorsed proposals" to the Food and Drug Administration; "set forth principles" and "urged" programs; it "expressed interest."[17] Nor did the Council live up to the expectations of those who had seen it as a chance for a real consumer voice in government. The *New Republic* labeled the Council as nothing more than a "group of prestigious consultants."[18] Indeed, the Council's *Report* was so bland that even business could dismiss it as a report that told President Kennedy "the same things he could have learned by reading the bulletins of such organizations as the Coop League."[19] After submitting its report in October, 1963, the Council did not meet again.

When President Johnson assumed office late in 1963, he lost no time in identifying his administration's interest in consumer problems. In a special message to Congress in February, 1964, Johnson described his predecessor's program, with perhaps more hopefulness than accuracy, as "active representation of the consumer—and a loud, clear-channel voice—at the topmost levels of government."[20] He announced the formation of the President's Committee on Consumer Interests, to be composed of the members of a new Consumer Advisory Council, together with the previously designated departmental and agency assistants for consumer affairs. To act as chairman of the new committee, Johnson appointed a Presidential special assistant for consumer affairs.

In its *Report* issued in 1966,[21] the second Consumer Advisory Council saw the need for further safeguards for the consumer's economic interests. The Council again identified as the major problems of consumers the same concerns so long associated with the consumer movement—consumer education, standards and labels, and consumer representation. In addition, the Council dealt with consumer problems in the particular area of home maintenance and repair, automobiles, health services, and textiles. It emphasized the consumer's problem in "shopping for goods and services," rather than in the larger problems such as antitrust and monetary and fiscal policies which were, in the Council's words, "behind the market." The Council recommended greater efforts for consumer education, particularly in consumer programs for low-income groups, and work toward standards for consumer goods. The Council emphasized the need for consumer representation in government and recommended the establishment of a "Joint Committee on Consumer Interests" to be "patterned after" the Congressional Joint Economic Committee.[22]

Consumer groups could be delighted at the report's findings, but nearly every segment of the business world could find in the report a threat of further government interference in the economy. One businessman, for example, claimed that "the Consumer Advisory Council has issued a little book . . . that has—in the aggregate—the explosive power of a nuclear bomb."[23] As it turned out, however, the Council's efforts came to nothing. Though the report was sent to the President in June, 1966, it was not released by the White House until nearly six months later and then without comment. Without Presidential backing or the pressure of an effective consumer lobby, there were no means to implement the Council's recommendations. The second Consumer Advisory Council had fared little better than the first.

As it turned out, the one "loud, clear-channel voice at the topmost levels of government" within the President's Committee on Consumer Interests was its Chairman, the President's first special assistant for consumer affairs. Esther Peterson, an Assistant Secretary of Labor, was appointed to the consumer post in early 1964. Her energy and outspokenness during the following three years brought business opposition and public attention to consumer issues long abandoned except by a devoted few. *Printer's Ink*, for example, editorialized that Mrs. Peterson represented a "pernicious threat to advertising" and "would destroy advertising as it exists today."[24]

Under the directives given her by the President, Mrs. Peterson undertook a variety of tasks. Soon after assuming her position, she organized, with the help of local consumer-minded groups, four regional conferences to try to find out what were "consumer problems." The programs were centered around the problems of money, health, housing, and food shopping. In her report to the President on these conferences, Mrs. Peterson pointed out that what consumers seemed to want most was information.[25] Consumers, she noted, wanted not only information for "rational consumer choices" about goods but also the broader kind of information involved in communication among consumers, business, and government together with the kind of information provided through consumer education in junior and senior high schools. In particular, she asserted the "urgent need for more and better informational and educational programs [for] persons with limited incomes, the elderly, the non-English speaking and the poorly educated."

In early 1967, Mrs. Peterson returned to her job in the Labor Department. It was suggested that she had been "released" as special assistant because her forthright espousal of consumers offended business interests. Betty Furness, a one-time television personality, was appointed to take her place. The appointment was generally considered to be a sop to business, but during her time in office, Miss Furness became progressively more outspoken on matters in the consumer's interest.[a]

When Richard M. Nixon became President, he appointed Mrs. Virginia Knauer, former head of Philadelphia's office of Consumer Protection, as his special assistant for consumer affairs. She continued to serve under President

---

[a]In recent years she has become closely associated with consumer affairs in New York City.

Ford. Mrs. Knauer's primary responsibilities have been to speak for the consumer interest in hearings on bills before Congress and to serve as the locus of consumer interests in the Administration. Her office receives thousands of consumer complaints, and as far as it is possible she works to set up industry-sponsored complaint resolution procedures. She also organizes conferences, conducts investigations, promotes consumer education, and coordinates federal consumer-protection activities. Mrs. Knauer herself makes numerous speeches, holds press conferences, and generally makes herself highly visible as the consumer's ally in Washington.

Mrs. Knauer's position has been a curious one. She has no specific authority; at the same time, in a Republican Administration, she has been able to be outspoken about the need for greater consumer protection. In the deliberation over the 1974 House proposed bill to create a consumer-protection agency, Mrs. Knauer urged passage of the legislation in opposition to the Administration's position that it should not be passed. She has not, however, been as supportive of a very strong bill as consumer advocates would like.[26]

Consumer Protection in State Government[b]

The growing initiative on consumer matters in the federal government has been paralleled by increasing attention to consumer protection at the level of state government. Historically, states have assumed responsibility for the maintenance of standard weights and measures, for seeing that food distributed within a state is pure and wholesome, and for prohibiting the sale of harmful drugs. States are also responsible for protecting consumers in cases of fraud in intrastate trade and for the intrastate regulation of public utilities, insurance,[c] banking, and money-lending, and for occupational licensing. State regulation is enforced and supervised by an array of regulatory agencies and, in the case of criminal fraud, by various prosecuting authorities. This pattern of legislation, both criminal and regulatory, has only recently come to be generally recognized as a body of consumer laws. Consumer advocates have realized that, rather than total reliance on the federal government, better enforcement of existing state laws, as well as the enactment of new laws aimed at specific consumer problems, can bring about more effective consumer protection.

This new interest in what state governments can do in the way of consumer protection is in contrast to the attitude of the early consumer movement. There is little indication that consumer advocates in the thirties gave much attention

---

[b]In the literature, most consumer measures at the national level are termed "consumer legislation." At the state level, however, they are nearly always spoken of as "consumer protection."

[c]In this case, at the invitation of Congress.

to what might be done by state or local governments to help consumers. At least two explanations can be given for this. One is that many of the new pressures on consumers—advertising, mass production, and mass selling—were nationwide in their effect. The other is that the New Deal recovery programs provided new and promising opportunities for work on consumer problems at the federal rather than the state level of government.

Several interrelated factors appear to be at work to produce this increased activity on behalf of consumers at the state level during the past fifteen years. The widely publicized Congressional investigations and debates, the Presidential consumer messages and appointments, and the political pressures suggested previously have revealed new opportunities and needs for state action. The civil rights movement and the national concern for poverty have brought attention to the problems of low-income and minority consumers. Political awareness of consumers has generated an increasing number of state consumer laws and agencies.

Nevertheless, consumer advocates maintain that there is much to be done at the state level toward more effective regulation and enforcement in the consumer's interest. They point out that consumer problems, as often as not, involve abuses that are already subject to state laws. Thus the lack of consumer protection has been a matter of official neglect rather than the absence of state government authority to do anything about it. To say that fraudulent practices are subject to already existing state laws, they suggest, is not sufficient to protect the consumer if he is unaware of the remedy available to him or of the procedures necessary to get a remedy. Information has to be brought to the attention of the responsible state official, usually the attorney general. The attorney general may be hesitant to prosecute because of the involved nature of a criminal case. In any event prosecution is a time-consuming procedure and is of little help to the already injured consumer. Consumer advocates also point out that state protection for consumers has suffered from the division of responsibility of consumer matters among state agencies, programs, and laws.

No two states have followed exactly the same pattern in efforts to raise the level of consumer protection. From state to state, however, the activities in consumer legislation and representation are similar enough that it is not necessary to examine individual states to convey the scope of these consumer programs. In the early 1960s, only half a dozen predominantly urban states had significant consumer programs, but the situation has been changing rapidly. By 1973, all states had at least one consumer office or division within another state office, and, by 1975, only Alabama and Georgia were without "broad consumer protection statutes."[27] And in New York State, for example, the number of state consumer offices and jurisdictions is already such that there has been some effort to establish a single agency to be responsible for all state consumer-protection activities.[28] A number of cities and counties also have special consumer offices.

State activities have concentrated on the protection and rights of redress for the individual consumer. Instead of focusing on a broadly defined consumer interest, consumer advocates have been concerned with effective protection in areas where consumers are most subject to abuse. The most prominent issues are those of auto, home repair, television and other repair services, insurance, landlord-tenant relations, prescription drugs, and consumer credit. Abuses arising from deceptive advertising, referral sales, bait-and-switch advertising, and other "deals" arranged by high-pressure salespeople or "sharp operators" have also been subjects for attention. In particular, these abuses have been discussed as they relate to consumers among groups having low incomes and little education.

Forty-eight states have established consumer-protection divisions in the office of the state attorney general, in some cases by legislative authorization, and, in others, by administrative action on the part of the attorney general.[29] These are units charged with a special responsibility for enforcing the laws for the protection of consumers. They vary in size and authority from state to state. In 1972, for example, the Delaware office had a budget of less than $10,000, while the Illinois office had a budget of some $1,000,000.[30] Nevertheless, in general, the staff and authority of these consumer offices have continued to expand.

The purpose of these special offices has been to provide consumers with an easier and more effective way to deal with a whole range of consumer problems such as auto and television repair which in most cases involve only a few hundred dollars. Traditionally, common law has provided consumers with civil relief from fraud, but this entails individual initiative and, often, lengthy and expensive court procedure. As for local criminal fraud enforcement, the situation with regard to any particular consumer abuse may be complicated by the limited jurisdictions of various district attorneys. Giving responsibility for consumer protection to the attorney general has the effect of substituting statewide governmental action for privately initiated claims and suits. The prestige and authority, not to say political benefits, of state action are such that relief for the consumer may be accomplished more quickly and with surer results than through a private court action or local criminal proceedings.

Counties, and in some cases, cities, have also established specialized agencies for dealing with consumer problems. New York City has had a Department of Consumer Affairs since 1969. The Department has been given authority for all laws that have to do with the sale of goods and services within the city. It has responsibility for both consumer protection and education.[31] And in Denver the district attorneys from the five metropolitan counties have set up a joint consumer office, funded by a Law Enforcement Assistance Administration block grant. The office is to deal with "economic crime." The largest number of cases reported concern new auto sales and repair and landlord-tenant relationships and involve less than five hundred dollars. The consumer office reports that about a third of the cases handled are successfully mediated.[32]

The passage of new laws designed to meet specific consumer problems is another general area of state activity for consumers. Such laws provide for the regulation of credit extended through finance companies, credit on automobile purchases, terms of repossession of durable goods being bought on installment payments, door-to-door sales, dance and health studio contracts, travel agents, and trade school and proprietary colleges. Forty-eight states now have some form of "deceptive trade act." While the kinds of consumer purchases regulated under these new laws are not necessarily new, rising incomes and changing economic and social conditions have brought these purchases within the reach of an increasing number of consumers; thus in the absence of specific regulation, greatly enlarging the opportunity for fraud and exploitation. To those who argue that general criminal sanctions are already available to prosecute such abuses, consumer advocates reply that these sanctions are "ineffective remedy in consumer fraud cases because of the difficulty and burdens inherent in criminal prosecutions."[33] The new consumer laws, according to consumer advocates, are more flexible and thus more effective in protecting consumers.[34]

A number of states have set up consumer representatives in the executive branch. The arrangements for these consumer representatives differ somewhat from state to state, but their purpose is generally the same—to articulate "the consumer view at the highest level of state government." Consumer representatives typically appear in behalf of the consumer at legislative and regulatory hearings on matters where the consumer interest would be affected. They coordinate the consumer activities of various governmental programs and agencies. They suggest areas where consumer protection is ineffective or inadequate. They serve as a focus of the consumer interest to both the public and to government. In spite of a broad range of responsibility, consumer representatives generally have no specific authority delegated to them, and their effectiveness depends on the particular representative's own ability to advance the consumer's cause.

The state of Pennsylvania provides a good example of what a forceful consumer advocate can accomplish at the state level. Herbert S. Denenberg was appointed Insurance Commissioner of Pennsylvania in 1971. The next year his Department published *A Shopper's Guide to Insurance*. It was quite literally a "shopper's guide," quoting companies, policies, and prices. There was understandably heavy opposition from the insurance industry, as the *Guide* opened the way for consumers to do comparative shopping in an area long restricted to experts. Denenberg withstood industry opposition and has gone on to be a forthright exponent of the "consumer's interest" in insurance and in other areas as well. He points out that in regulatory hearings, at both national and state levels, "industry's point of view is always heard and . . . the consumer's point of view is rarely if ever heard."[33] He maintains that consumers have the right to be heard and the right to the kind of information on which to make rational decisions. In his view state governments can experiment in ways that are not open to the federal government. He argues that consumer protection at the state level can be both more innovative and more useful than at the national level.

It is difficult to assess the effectiveness of and extent to which consumers have benefited from this variety of state consumer-protective activity. The discretion of the particular state attorney general, whose term in office is usually subject to the vote of the state electorate, determines the vigor with which any consumer division in his office operates. Consumer laws in nearly all states have tended to concentrate on a narrow range of consumer transactions that are subject to fraud and "sharp operators." Moreover, in any state, the mere existence of a specific agency or law, however ineffective, can be a substitute for more general action in the consumer's behalf. The same kinds of opposition to consumer measures which are voiced in Congressional hearings also show up at the state level where, if anything, they have more relative weight. Yet the past decade has seen real growth in state government activity on behalf of consumers. Despite their uneven quality, consumer-protection measures have changed, in the words of one California legislator, from being "turkeys" to causes as unassailable as motherhood.[36]

5

Ralph Nader: Virtuoso of the Consumer Movement

*[Business] depredations are part of a raging corporate radicalism which gener-
ates technological violence, undermines the integrity of government, breaks laws,
blocks needed reforms, and repudiates a quality-competitive system with substantial consumer sovereignty.*

Ralph Nader (December 1970)

So spectacular has Ralph Nader been as an advocate of the consumer's cause
that many people identify him and his work as the sum and substance of the
consumer movement. From the publication of his *Unsafe at Any Speed* in
late 1965 and his subsequent battle with General Motors Corporation, Nader's
name has become synonymous with consumerism and with efforts to control the power of corporate enterprise—both private and public—over the individual citizen and consumer. Nader's zeal, and that of his small group of col-
laborators, is credited with the increasing awareness and publicity for consumer issues and with much of the consumer legislation passed by Congress
in the past decade. Nader's attacks on business and on a government which,
in his view, serves business rather than the public have had an almost religious
character, and he has been variously pictured as a David against Goliath, a
medieval crusader, and a Luther posting his theses. In all of this, Nader has
been seen as the champion of consumers against the forces that deny them
the rights and benefits that should be theirs in, to use Nader's frequently re-
curring term, a "just" society.

Nader and his work have, undoubtedly, done more than anything else in
recent times to publicize the consumer movement and to give momentum to its
efforts in behalf of consumers. And, like the consumer movement, Nader defines
the consumer's interest as that which results when there is a freely competitive
economy and producers must necessarily respond to consumer demand. The
difference between Nader and the consumer movement lies in the fact that
Nader's view of what needs to be done to achieve an economy that can fulfill
its promise to consumers is as concerned with citizens as with consumers; the
changes Nader calls for go far beyond those usually advocated by the consumer
movement. Even so, Nader's view of the economy is as unrealistic as that of
the consumer movement and similarly limiting with respect to the kind of
change that is possible.

Nader's Attack on Consumer Problems

Nader first appeared on the consumer scene as a one-man crusade against the automobile industry. Working almost entirely on his own, Nader collected information with which he put together a scathing attack on the hazards of the design and workmanship of American automobiles. In his *Unsafe at Any Speed*, Nader charged that the automobile manufacturers put sales and profits ahead of safety as they "deliberately held low . . . consumer's expectations regarding automobile innovation."[1] He asserted that, through the Automobile Safety Foundation, the manufacturers managed to get the emphasis on safety focused on the driver and the highway, rather than on the vehicle itself. Nader concluded that a major cause of highway death and injury was the automobile itself and that only government intervention could make manufacturers responsible for safe design and thus "free millions of human beings from unnecessary mutilation."[2]

In the spring of 1965, just prior to the publication of Nader's book, Senator Abraham Ribicoff announced that a subcommittee of the Senate Governmental Operations Committee would hold hearings on automobile safety. Ribicoff called on Nader to assist with the subcommittee's preparations for the summer hearings. At the hearings, the primary issue was what efforts the automobile companies were making to design and produce safer vehicles. In a now-famous exchange, Senator Robert Kennedy, who was a member of the subcommittee, was able to extract from the president of General Motors the information, that in the previous year, General Motors' expenditures on its safety program had totaled less than one and a half million dollars at a time when its profits had reached more than one and a half billion dollars.

The cause of automobile safety acquired another dimension in what appeared to be General Motors' underhanded response to the criticism of its product. Early in 1966, Nader charged that General Motors had hired private detectives to try to get information about him that would discredit him and his book. In these circumstances Nader appeared not only as the advocate of safer automobiles but as a righteous David against the Goliath of the largest corporation in the United States. In the ensuing publicity, James M. Roche, then president of General Motors, made a public apology to Nader. Later, however, Nader filed a 27 million dollar suit against General Motors for invasion of privacy. It was settled before going to trial for something less than 500 thousand dollars.

With these events, public attention on automobile safety heightened, and Congress passed the National Traffic and Vehicle Safety Act in March 1966, less than a year after the hearings had begun.[a] This legislation authorized the establishment of the Highway Traffic Safety Administration to be responsible for mandating safety standards for automobiles and new and used tires. It also

---

[a]Hearings on automotive safety had been held during the 1960s by Congressman Kenneth Roberts, but these generated little publicity or results.

specified procedures for the recall of defective vehicles. The Administration has now promulgated some thirty or more standards for automobiles, including dual braking systems and over-the-shoulder and interlocking seat belts in the front seat. The 1966 legislation is credited with being "the first time that the automobile industry had succumbed to any legislation" and a "breakthrough issue" in consumer legislation in Congress.[3]

Automobile safety was the first in what has come to be a series of crusades by Nader against conditions in the American economy which he sees as destructive of the rights of consumers. In the years since 1966, Nader's energies have been expended in so many directions that it is difficult to categorize them, but his investigations and calls for action can be divided into several rather general areas. Nader has dealt with the prevention of unsafe and harmful products from coming onto the market. Along these lines he has been concerned with the problem of pollution in both its environmental and human health aspects. Nader has also attacked federal agencies for their disregard of the public interest in their failure to carry out the responsibilities assigned them. And, finally, he has worked to expose the abuse of the consumer and citizen in a wide variety of matters like pension reform, the treatment of the aged and mentally ill, and even Congress itself. Overarching all of Nader's efforts is his belief that the base cause of these problems is the power and greed of corporate enterprise in America.

In the area of unsafe and harmful products, Nader wrote a series of articles for *The New Republic* and made personal appearances in cities across the country in which he detailed the filthy conditions in state-regulated packing plants not subject to federal inspection. His efforts are credited with the public pressure which enabled the passage of the Wholesome Meat Act of 1967. Nader is also given credit for the 1968 passage of the Natural Gas Pipeline Safety Act and the Radiation Control for Health and Safety Act. The latter grew out of Nader's investigations into the dangers of the indiscriminate use of x-ray for routine medical and dental examinations. Likewise the Coal Mine Health and Safety Act of 1969, which resulted from Nader's investigation into the responsibilities of the Bureau of Mines for miners' health, and the Comprehensive Occupational Safety and Health Act of 1970 are linked with Nader's name. Nader's endeavor to get *all* smoking banned from airplanes was unsuccessful, but the provision of non-smoking sections was a direct outcome of that endeavor. Nader's most recent effort is directed against the dangers of nuclear power plants. He seeks to prevent the construction of any more such plants on the grounds that there is, at the present time, no assurance that there will be no accidents inside the plants that might endanger wide areas surrounding the plants.[4]

This same concern for the ability of American industry to foist off onto consumers dangerous and unhealthful products has led Nader to expose the role of business enterprise in creating the high levels of air and water pollution now apparent throughout many sections of the United States. In *Vanishing Air* (1970) and in *Water Wasteland* (1971), Nader's study groups have reported the extent to which businesses have ignored the problems created by industrial production in fouling air and water. The theme running through these accusations is that business has profited from this pollution. By neglecting to clean up after itself (Nader's phrase is"toilet train"), Nader claims that business has reduced its costs and increased its profits at the expense of the environment and the consumer.

Equally as significant as his accusations directly against business has been Nader's campaign to force federal regulatory agencies to carry out the statutory responsibilities assigned to them. Agencies like the Federal Trade Commission and the Food and Drug Administration were established to see to it that, in certain areas like advertising and harmful drugs, business did not act in a way that was contrary to the consumer's interest. Nader's position is that, instead of protecting the consumer's interest, these agencies have become, at best, dilatory in their actions, and, at worst, the pawns of business. In a scathing report released early in 1969, Nader charged that the FTC delayed in following up on complaints, depended on "voluntary codes instead of rigorous prosecution" and often played a "hands off" game with major corporations.[5] The report resulted in President Nixon's setting up a study of the FTC by a panel of the American Bar Association. The panel concurred with Nader's criticisms. The result of this was a shake-up in the staff of the FTC and a "new vigilance" on the part of the agency.[6] A year later, a similar investigation into the FDA uncovered the agency's failure to recognize the possible dangers of cyclamates and monosodium glutamates as food additives. The publicity given this by the press brought about the FDA's banning of cyclamates from soft drinks and the voluntary decision by baby foods manufacturers to stop adding monosodium glutamate to all their products. Nader has called the FDA a "shameful handmaiden to a food industry that pollutes our food supply . . . and to pharmaceutical companies which sell useless and/or harmful drugs."[7]

In recent years, Nader has diligently lobbied for a permanent federal consumer agency that would be empowered to present the consumer's interest before the regulatory agencies. In Nader's view, such representation would assure a hearing for consumers and would prevent the agencies and the industries they regulate from taking actions that profit business at the expense of the consumer. Such an agency, Nader feels, would be a watchdog for consumers and an effective way of assuring that regulatory agencies do not become pawns to corporate power.

In other areas Nader and his coworkers have written a number of exhaustive reports exposing the extent to which private and public enterprise abuse their responsibilities to consumers and to society. In *Damning the West* (1973) Nader's associates accused the Bureau of Reclamation of expensive and unnecessary construction of dams and irrigation systems that serve the interests of the rich and powerful to the detriment of the poor and weak. *Old Age, The Last*

Segregation (1971) attacked the nursing-home industry, accusing it of greed in preying on the sick and aged in pursuit of profit. In *Sowing the Wind* (1972), a Nader study group investigated the relationship between agricultural and business interests which, particularly in their use of chemicals, profited at the expense of small farmers and the environment.

Nader's ability to forge ahead on so many different fronts during the past ten years can be accounted for partly by the staff he has attracted to work with him. Drawn by his zeal, many college and law school students have participated in his drive to right the wrongs he sees perpetrated on the individual American consumer. Upaid students, dubbed "Nader's Raiders," did most of the investigation of the FTC and the FDA. Starting in 1965 as a one-man attack on automobile safety, Nader's operation now has several dozen different specialized groups. So large has Nader's operation become that it has been termed a "conglomerate." In 1969, Nader set up the Center for the Study of Responsive Law, a tax-exempt body to do educational and investigative research. With grants from Carnegie and several smaller foundations, Nader's study groups carried out painstaking investigations into a large number of areas. The Center is now engaged, for example, in a systematic study of consumer complaints. This is an effort to determine what are the most frequent kinds of consumer complaints and what is an effective and systematic way to handle them.

Because of its tax-exempt status, the Center was unable to carry on any political activity. In 1970, Nader, using his own money, largely that won from his suit against General Motors, established the Public Interest Research Group (PIRG) for the purpose of carrying on such activity. Nader saw the PIRG as an "action organization" where he and his fellow workers could participate in court actions and in Congressional hearings.[8] A year later Nader launched a nationwide organization known as "Public Citizen" to raise financial support for his advocacy role. Nader is president of this organization which raises most of its funds through direct-mail solicitation of memberships at 15 dollars a year. The first drive raised nearly a million dollars,[9] and the organization claims contributions from over 158,000 people.

Public Citizen has become the central focus of Nader-guided action. Through its Congress Watch, Public Citizen, in the words of a mailing, "is urging Congress to bring about reformed procedures and get our national legislature down to the business of representing the people, instead of weaving silken rhetoric." The mailing specifically cites "effective energy price and anti-monopoly measures" to "reduce the crushing burden" of fuel prices, and health insurance and energy conservation measures as areas of concern and pressure through lobbying. Other Public Citizen activities include litigation before the courts and regulatory agencies and health care research. Public Citizen activities are action- rather than research-oriented. Through state and local Citizen Action Groups and Public Interest Research Groups, especially on college and university campuses, Nader-type activities are decentralized throughout the country.

Nader's Perspectives on the American Economy

Nader sees corporate power as responsible for most of what is wrong with the American economy today. In its abuse of individual consumers, in its manipulation of government to its own purposes, in its disregard for the disadvantaged groups in society, and in its neglect of the nation's social and physical environment, the power of big business is seen by Nader as a radical movement, undermining the long-accepted American values of a just society based on individual responsibilities and rights. In answer to charges that he is himself a radical, seeking to destroy the "American system," Nader responds that business is the real destroyer of the system as it undercuts market and consumer power.[10]

Nader charges that "corporations, by their control of both the market and government, have been able to divert scarce resources to uses that have little human benefit or are positively harmful."[11] He calls these wasted resources "involuntary expenditures" on the part of consumers. The corporation, in effect, causes consumers to spend in ways they would not rationally choose. Nader details the ways corporations are able to bilk the public and increase their own power and profitability.[12] Corporations, he maintains, make people pay for poor and worthless goods. As examples, he cites short weights in packaging, worthless drugs advertised and sold as useful, and low-speed automobile-collision damage that could be eliminated by effective bumper design. He maintains that consumers have to pay for the costs imposed by market concentration which eliminates competition, increases prices, and inhibits change that would be beneficial to the consumer. In Nader's view, consumers must also bear the costs of "compulsory consumption" of air and water pollution, unsafe food additives, and dangerous workplaces. Nader accuses corporations of what he calls "corporate socialism", whereby through tax loopholes, outright corruption and manipulation of expenditures, business is able to subsidize itself through the transfer of large amounts of public funds.[13] Finally, Nader points to poor people whose consumption is restricted by the higher prices they have to pay for the goods they are able to buy and by the harsh penalties imposed on them by monetary and tax policies that favor the rich over the poor.

Nader is highly critical of advertising, much of which he sees as having "abandoned its purpose of providing product or service information" and as giving consumers "little more than fictitious information with which they make wrong choices."[14] Thus to Nader, much of advertising is an "enormous waste to consumers." In Nader's view, advertising, which entices customers to products through deceptive blandishments or packaging, subverts the consumer's ability to compare price and quality. In a 1969 study, Nader and Aileen Coward requested substantiation for advertising claims from fifty-eight companies whose advertising included what they called "vague and unclear" statements.[15] Of the fifty-eight companies, sixteen did not reply, three replied with clinical studies which Nader thought were of "dubious value," one company retracted an advertising claim, and the rest responded to the request for substantiation in what

Nader and Coward considered to be a superficial or otherwise unsatisfactory way. The results of the study were submitted as a petition to the FTC in 1970. Within months, the FTC called for supporting data for the advertising claims from a number of companies cited in the Nader-Coward study. Later some companies were forced to publicly retract what the FTC determined to be false claims.

Nader has cited the advertising directed toward children as "particularly insidious." In the case of cereals and other pop foods, children, especially through Saturday morning television programming, are lured to much high-cost and sometimes nutritionally worthless food.

Nader reserves his most bitter invective for what he calls "corporate disregard for life" and "corporate-induced violence." This "violence" and "carnage" includes the cancer caused by smoking, the road deaths and injuries associated with unsafe cars, and the pain, suffering, and death resulting from burns caused by flammable fabrics. Nader cites the "innocent confidence" of the consumer that business strives to sell only safe products and that government, through regulation, prohibits the sale of unhealthful or of unsafe products. But the reality of all this, Nader maintains, is that companies ignore the violence and carnage for the sake of profits, and government regulatory agencies, because of their subservience to business, make only half-hearted attempts to force business to be responsive to consumers.

Nader also accuses corporate power and government compliance of subverting the nation's potential for economic growth from meeting "urgent human needs." For Nader, the resources spent on worthless and useless goods, on advertising, and on goods that are destructive of human life are resources not available for safer products, better health care, sharing with the poor, or restoring and maintaining environmental quality. He complains of "large aggregate economic growth" which is not matched by "commensurate growth in consumer value." He accuses business of a "balance sheet morality" which ignores "the values and pleas" not represented in such an accounting.[16]

In Nader's view, it is corporate power that has weakened and nearly destroyed the competitive fabric of American society. Nader's faith is in a fully competitive market economy that responds to the individual consumer and thus gives the consumer power. In a competitive market, business is accountable to consumers. To restore the American economy and American government to this kind of a system, Nader calls for policies that will break down the large concentrations of power now in the hands of business and government. Nader is torn between policies that will actually break up large corporations into a number of competing units and those that will secure the results of competition through regulation. But he sees the need for a diffusion of power to eliminate the authoritarian control of business over American life. He calls for a "deconcentration of corporate power" through intensified government antitrust and regulatory efforts and through federal chartering.

Nader insists that, by breaking up the large corporations into units that will have to compete with one another, they will be forced to submit to, rather than dominate, consumer choice. If there is effective competition, then "many industries would be displaced or diminished as superior technologies are invented and sold on their merits."[17] With effective competition, to use an example cited by Nader, a company like American Telephone and Telegraph could no longer force a customer to be totally dependent on it for communication and to pay the attendant high charges and resulting high profits guaranteed by such dependence. Nor with competition could companies continue to ignore the existence of safer products to protect their already-established lines. As examples of this corporate ability to avoid change from established and profitable ways of doing business, Nader cites pollution-free automobile engines and safe power lawn-mowers, for which he claims technologies are available.[18] Competition would, in Nader's view, limit price-fixing, worthless products, and the power of business in government.

In lieu of competition to force the accountability of business to the public interest, Nader calls for vigorous regulation of industry under the regulatory authorities set up to assure corporate accountability. Agencies like the Food and Drug Administration, the Federal Trade Commission, the Interstate Commerce Commission, the Civil Aeronautics Board, and the Environmental Protection Agency already have the authority to make business conform its activity to the public interest. Pressure brought to bear on the President and Congress is needed to free these bodies from the dominance of the industries they are supposed to regulate. As support for this view, Nader cites the action the FDA and the FTC took as a result of his investigation and prodding. Similarly, Nader contends that legislation in the public interest, once it is passed, is often allowed to go unenforced. He cites the unwillingness of the Department of Commerce to act under the power granted it in the Flammable Fabrics Act of 1967 to set standards for a variety of clothing and household products fabrics.[19] Where necessary, as in the case of automobile safety, Nader believes that additional regulatory power should be given to government. This is the case where "a burgeoning technology is giving corporations more power than they choose to exercise responsibly."[20]

In the federal chartering or licensing of corporations, Nader sees another way by which the abuses of the large corporation can be controlled.[21] For companies in interstate trade, Nader would require federal charters to be substituted for the different state charters under which United States companies now function. Nader points out that when incorporation first began in England in the sixteenth and seventeenth centuries and later in the United States, it was granted as a privilege and not as a right, and that corporations were seen as "performing public functions in the public interest."[22] But, according to Nader, this has changed so that now corporations are "granted more rights than responsibilities." Nader sees the competition among states in providing incorporation havens as bringing about the lowest common denominator in terms of public accountability of private businesses. Nader maintains that historically there has been a long discussion of federal chartering, but that it is only now, in his words, an "idea whose time has come." He notes that federal chartering has come to the fore during times of national concern about the power of large business, but that in the 1880s and in 1914, and then again toward the end of the Great Depression, the alternative of more effective regulation of business has been chosen over federal licensing. Now, he maintains, with the continuing growth of the large national and multinational corporation, states are no longer, if they ever were, able to exert sufficient power over organizations which, in terms of sheer size, dwarf the state itself.

While federal regulatory power is not the "one" solution to corporate power according to Nader, it can help to control that power in the public interest. Nader would establish a Federal Chartering Agency with the responsibility for licensing and regulating all companies in interstate trade. The charters would become a pact between the government, representing the public, and the corporation and would be conditional upon the corporation's continued service of the consumer's interest. Among the stipulations Nader would build into this pact are "strict" antitrust provisions, what he calls "corporate disclosure," to provide information about any and all aspects of corporate life that have a bearing on the public interest, and appropriate penalties for companies that do not discharge their public obligations. The overall effect of such federal chartering would be to "constitutionalize" corporations, to use Nader's terms. It would make "private aggregations of power," like states, subject to constitutional obligations. Such a move would, in Nader's words, prohibit "public power without public accountability."

In addition to federal chartering, he calls for continuing government policies that foster competition or otherwise work toward the results that would be brought about if there were effective competition.[23] Nader urges, for example, that governments at all levels use their enormous market power, as business's largest single customer, to raise the standards of consumer products. If governments would specify a pollution-free automobile as what they would purchase, Nader is convinced that in a short time a pollution-free automobile would be produced. Likewise governments should make available to consumers all the accumulated information about standards and specifications of products governments buy.

Nader also calls for changes in federal law that would allow class-action suits to be brought by consumers against businesses, even where damage to an individual consumer is quite small. Class-action suits can be filed now in federal courts if the individual claim is for more than 10,000 dollars, but this high figure is very limiting in terms of most consumer goods and services. (The dollar figure is not in effect where the suit charges corporate violation of antitrust laws.) Nader would reduce the limit to permit consumers to band together to seek redress for corporate wrongdoing. Opposition to such a measure is based on the grounds that it would subject corporations to thousands of nuisance suits. Nader, however, calls class-action suits a "terrific tool" for consumers.

Nader has been adamant on the point that wrongdoing on the part of corporate officials is criminal. In the category of wrongdoing, he includes, for example, the hazardous design defects in the Corvair automobile which he maintains were known to GM officials at the time the Corvair was marketed. Similarly, neglect of other standards of production set by government should subject corporate officials to criminal sanctions. Nader believes that "a federal law must be passed to include all products: one that will set the highest standards practical technology permits and that will subject willful violators to criminal penalties."[24] Nader contrasts the penalties imposed on "an automaker who builds a defective car that takes life" with those imposed on drivers "found guilty of gross negligence and manslaughter."[25] He holds that corporate–white-collar–crime is even more susceptible to control by criminal penalties than other kinds of crime because of the "unendurable public shame" connected with criminal penalties.

Finally, in his strategy for the "deconcentration of corporate power," Nader places great emphasis on the responsibility of the individual. In the final analysis the key to Nader's vision for a "just society" is individual action. Nader calls it a "new kind of citizenship." He calls for every American citizen to make the same commitment to action that he himself has made. People must develop a "sensitivity to injustice." Every citizen must be willing to investigate, to learn, and then to act against the "hazardous products, monopolistic practices, endlessly clever frauds, overpricing, and swindles" that "run rampant throughout the economy."[26] Within this framework of a kind of eternal vigilance, corporate and government power can be brought to social accountability. Not only can such vigilance bring about change in the sense of bringing to light new techniques for dealing with the social abuses of power, but it is also required for the continuing enforcement of gains already made—of regulations already designed and in force for the protection of the public interest.

Nader's notion of *action* is more than an awareness of the issues and being willing to vote correctly. Nader sees the need for personal involvement and personal commitment. It is here more than in any other area that Nader's almost religious-like vows to a cause show up most clearly. A *New Yorker* "Profile" gives an account of Nader's reaction to an autograph seeker following a lecture which Nader had concluded with a call for individual responsibility and action. Nader refused to sign the proffered program not on the basis of disdain but, rather, on the basis that asking for an autograph was a sad and discouraging response to a clarion call to join the cause.[27] Nader believes that the manager or worker who sees in the action of the corporation which employs him an abuse of the consumer or public interest should expose his employer.[28] Nader terms such a person an "ethical whistleblower" who "may be guided by the Golden Rule, a refusal to aid and abet crimes, occupational standards of ethics, or a genuine sense of patriotism."[29] For Nader this kind of on-the-job citizenship ". . . is a critical source of information, ideas, and suggestions for change."[30] Nader assumes that there will be the "protections of the law and supportive groups" for workers who do accept this kind of social responsibility.

Complementing this on-the-job citizenship, which, because of the numbers that might be involved, is potentially the most powerful force for change, are what Nader calls "full-time professional citizens" and "part-time professional citizens." The first are people like Nader himself who are "independently based" and who devote themselves to the task of "working *on* institutions to improve and reshape them or replace them with improved ways of achieving just missions."[31] These full-time professional citizens would also be available to organize the work of part-time professional citizens who, Nader points out, will more and more be working four-day weeks and for whom "involvement [in professional citizenship] can become an integral part of the good life."[32] Working together, these citizens can develop the processes by which they can undertake to deal with corporate abuse of the public interest. Such processes, Nader believes, will ". . . metabolize the latent will of people to contribute to their community and count as individuals rather than as cogs in large organizational wheels."[33]

Nader and the Consumer Movement

For the consumer movement, Ralph Nader is the most powerful and effective force it has had in its nearly fifty-year history. As a brilliant and effective spokesman and lobbyist for the consumer's cause, Nader has achieved during the last ten years an immense amount of publicity for the consumer and for consumer problems. He has testified numerous times each year before Congressional hearings, he writes and speaks for wide audiences, and he has had an excellent press. But Nader's "passion" for change far surpasses that envisioned by the consumer movement. Furthermore, Nader is less concerned with the consumer than with the citizen: The term "consumerism" is a pale image of Nader's analysis of the extent of the control of corporate enterprise over American life. Nader's goal is for a structural change in society that will achieve participatory democracy in economic as well as in political matters.

There is, however, much in Nader's view of the economy and of the consumer's role in the economy that is consistent with that of the consumer movement. Like the consumer movement, Nader sees the free market as the best guarantee of consumer protection. Again and again in his tirades against business, Nader speaks of the destruction of the market by corporate power and of how, without effective competition, the corporation is unrestrained in the manipulation of resources toward its own ends. His position, like that of the consumer movement, is that the consumer's best interests can be served in an economy of competing firms, accountable through competition only to consumers. Nader's arguments against corporate profits suggest his belief that a return to genuine competition would push profits to the zero-level which obtains in the theoretical model of competition. To emphasize his point about freely competing markets and prices, Nader cites a Federal Trade Commission study that estimates that where there is significant concentration in an industry, prices are some 25 percent higher than they would be if the industry were broken up into smaller, competing firms.[34]

Nader has stood with the consumer movement in its concern for a whole array of consumer problems: in truth in packaging and in lending and in the various pieces of legislation designed to remove unsafe and unhealthful products from the market. And Nader's voice has given great strength to the consumer movement's efforts to get Congressional approval of legislation establishing an independent consumer agency in the federal government. Furthermore, in a movement that is otherwise rather amorphous, Nader has been a person that consumers could identify with. Consumers see in him a way by which their own problems are being recognized and dealt with.

In three other areas are Nader and the consumer movement in close agreement. Like the consumer movement Nader sees advertising as demeaning and destructive of consumer sovereignty. "Deception through advertising," he claims, "reaches all segments of society." Consumers are tricked into buying goods which they would otherwise recognize as being poor quality or harmful or worthless. Nader also stands four-square with the consumer movement on the matter of consumer information. He believes that the kind of information that would be useful to consumers in determining value based on price and quality is withheld from them. In fact, according to Nader, corporations "go to fantastic lengths to avoid competition over value." They substitute for information advertising and other deceptive devices, such as stamps and coupons, to divert consumers from purposeful consideration of price and quality. Like the consumer movement, Nader sees informed consumers as "one of the touchstones of the market system." To bring about such informed consumers, Nader calls for computer centers in supermarket areas so that consumers can have available to them the specific information about price and quality of all the various goods they buy and then be able to make intelligent decisions based on value comparisons among competing goods.

Finally, Nader, like the consumer movement, builds on the conflict between business and consumers. For Nader, the "consumer and the corporation [are] bitter enemies,"[35] and consumer protection and corporate responsibility are "two sides of the same coin." The key to consumer protection is either dissolution or management of corporate power. For this reason it is probably Nader, as much as any part of the consumer movement, that has in recent times raised the ire of business against consumerism. It is also true that Nader has forced business to take steps to counter the rising tide of consumer unrest which he has been responsible for generating.

Nader, however, has been increasingly critical of the consumer movement. He acknowledges that, for a long time (in fact until he came along), the consumer movement stood virtually alone in its efforts to make the economy responsive to consumer interests. But he also recognizes that its achievement was limited to the development of "an awareness among consumers that they [were] being gypped and endangered."[36] What is needed now, says Nader, is "the economic and political machinery" to control the corporate power that is the source of consumer abuse. To Nader, awareness is not enough; the real issue is action. And it is over this issue that Nader and the longer-standing elements of the consumer movement have disagreed.

In 1967, Nader became a member of the Board of Directors of Consumers Union. Two years later, CU set up a Washington office to monitor consumer legislation and to help organize consumer pressure on Congress. Peter H. Schuck, who was appointed to head the Washington office, had been a former associate of Nader's. But Nader has been increasingly critical of what he sees as CU's reluctance to move more forcefully as a consumer advocate, and, in mid-1975, Nader resigned from Consumers Union charging that he could "better use the ten days a year spent on CU matters in other pursuits within the consumer movement. . . ."[37] He asserted, and indeed CU's executive director concurred, that CU's primary interest was in testing products. From Nader's point of view this is too limited an agenda for the consumer movement.

This basic difference between Nader and the consumer movement is never more evident than in their respective views of the content and role of consumer education. The consumer movement's approach to consumer education is to stress the importance of the *consumer's* responsibility in acquiring knowledge about goods. The consumer needs to be informed about ways by which unscrupulous businesses can take advantage of him, and to resist the blandishments of advertising by ascertaining his own value systems of what are worthwhile expenditures in order to achieve the outcomes that would be guaranteed if competition did exist. For the consumer movement, consumer education is to help consumers change in order to make the system work as if competition existed. For Nader, however, it is not consumers, but the system, that must change. In this view, consumer education is to make consumers understand "the obligations . . . companies have to their customers, their workers, and to the government agencies which regulate them."[38] For Nader, consumer education is to show consumers how they can change the system; consumer education is "the bridge between knowing and doing."

This dividing of the ways between Nader and other elements of the consumer movement may raise problems within the movement. Nader has been able to do what the consumer movement has not been able to do—he has raised money to support the cause and he has brought about change. Probably even more important, Nader has been able to generate a level of enthusiasm and publicity for the consumer that is far greater than at any time before he came on the scene. The consumer movement is dependent on Nader for its continuing vitality. Ralph Nader, on the other hand, is not dependent on the consumer movement. Where they share concerns, Nader appears willing to be considered a part of the movement. Where they do not, his own personal goals come first.

Nader's Critics

As would be expected, the most vehement criticism of Nader comes from the defenders of a laissez-faire policy on the part of government toward business. This is the same world of corporate power he most strenuously attacks. In the view of business, Nader gives misinformation about business and the power of business, and he proposes tactics that are ineffective to deal with consumer problems and that may in the end seriously weaken the fabric of American society.

Business criticizes Nader for his exaggerated and deceptive claims about the extent and consequences of corporate power. It is said that Nader vastly over-estimates the level of profits of American business. In reiterating a statistic of Senator Philip A. Hart that, in 1969, $200 billion of personal spending represented worthless expenditure on the part of consumers, Nader implies that this amount became a part of corporate profit. In fact, say pro-business sources, this amount represents about five times the amount of all profits in the United States.[39] Similarly, business charges that Nader does not understand that the costs of higher quality and/or safer products or greater environmental control will ultimately be reflected in the price of the product rather than, as Nader sees it, in lower levels of business profits.

Business also feels that Nader is proposing the wrong solutions to the problems he identifies. The charge most often made against Nader is that, in seeking increased government regulation of business, he will impose on consumers even greater costs than he thinks he is saving them. The pursuit of quality products through regulation, business points out, will mean that low-quality and low-price products will disappear from the market. The imposition of the costs of faulty products on to business will not only raise the prices of all products but will discourage consumers from buying good-quality products. This will result because consumers know any damages they sustain through poor-quality products will not be borne by themselves but will be subsidized by all other purchasers of that particular product. The point is often made that the more expensive, if safer, products will work a special hardship on people with low incomes.

With regard to Nader's proposal for federal chartering, it is charged that such a step would prohibit corporations from responding to the genuine market demands of consumers who decide to buy or not to buy the product. Instead of being able to produce, for example, the kinds of cars that consumers want, the corporation would be forced, through its federal charter, to respond to the nonmarket demands of those who think they know what kind of car the corporation *ought* to produce.[40] It is also charged that, if in an attempt to limit corporate growth, federal chartering would prohibit multiproduct companies, then this, in fact, would impair the ability of one company to produce and compete with the product produced by another company. The result, in the end, would be to reinforce the monopoly power of individual companies.[41] Without any foreseeable benefits from federal chartering, it becomes, in the words of one, "another in a long series of proposals to coerce people to do what they do not want to do."[42]

Probably the most often-cited industry criticism of Nader's proposals is that the increased regulation which he proposes will not only increase the costs of products produced in highly concentrated industries, but, most importantly, it will not be effective. In words matching Nader's, Milton Friedman condemns the regulatory agencies as "alphabetical monstrosities preying on consumers from their privileged sanctuaries in Washington."[43] To support this criticism, industry defenders cite the long history of government regulation and its failure to achieve more than heightened concentration, as in the radio and television broadcasting industry or protected inefficiency, as in the case of the railroads.[44] Business insists that open competition between businesses is the most effective regulator of prices and profits and the best guarantee of the consumer's interest. In Friedman's words, "imperfect as it is, the market does a better job of protecting the consumer than does the political process."[45]

In contrast to the rather solid front business presents with regard to the issue of regulation, there is something of a split with regard to the question of the proposed consumer-protection agency in the federal government. Some opponents maintain that no agency can represent the diverse interests of more than 200 million consumers and that this will result in the head of the agency becoming a "consumer czar," with power to determine what consumers want. Ronald Reagan has called the proposed agency a device that would only "please . . . professional consumerists who thrive on finding more ways to tighten the federal vise" on individual lives. The *Wall Street Journal* editorialized that such an agency would help "very little" and that the "underlying premise" of the act to establish the agency was less consumer-oriented than it was "anti-business."[46] Spokesmen for some large corporations like Montgomery Ward, Mobil Oil, and Polaroid, however, have testified in Congressional hearings in support of the establishment of a consumer-protection agency,[47] probably on the assumption that it may be easier to deal with one consumer agency than with consumer responsibility scattered throughout the dozens of federal agencies.

Probably business's most deeply felt criticism of Nader is that he is out to destroy business and the free-enterprise system. One commentator includes Nader in the "so-called consumer groups" which "have as their ultimate goal breaking up the corporate structure of this country."[48] Many see Nader and his followers, who have "built a fire under the pot of consumer discontent to the boiling point . . .," as the source of the increasing level of antibusiness sentiment in the United States during the past six or eight years.[49] They believe that Nader's charges against business have given "people's complaints . . . an audible voice which has turned a large segment of our population against the whole business structure."[50]

From a different perspective, Nader can also be criticized for his ambivalence toward technology. On the one hand, he criticizes business for not incorporating technology into products like computerized information, which will be of use to consumers. Similarly, he maintains that industry resists the use of available technology to deal with problems of safer products and a cleaner environment. On the other hand, Nader resists the implications of a technology that brings about increased specialization and a division of labor that requires increasingly large units of production. The ability to break up corporate enterprise is dependent on the ability to assure an equally efficient output at the smaller scale of production. While there are some who suggest that this is possible, the increasing scale of production in noncapitalist countries, as well as in capitalist countries, is evidence that scale is a requirement of technology rather than politics.[51] If such is the case, then action to bring about a dissolution of corporate power can do little to increase the output of high-quality products at a lower price.

Nor does Nader analyze the effect of his program on the distribution of income. Implicit in his argument for structural change in the power of corporate enterprise is the notion that smaller profits to business, based on lower prices to consumers, will bring about a significant redistribution of income. Without explicitly saying that corporate power is the reason for low incomes, Nader does suggest that alternate corporate disregard and then abuse of poor people and minorities, along with governmental waste of tax dollars in terms of both goods produced and workers hired, is a central element in the problem of poverty.[52] While it is difficult to estimate what would be the distributional effects of a break-up of the large corporations, it would probably not eradicate poverty in this country. Furthermore, it can be argued that Nader's program to force enterprise to move from its present patterns of production toward a more "rational" pattern could be viewed by poor people as a move to deny them, in the future, the outpourings of consumer goods that have been available in the past to higher income, and more fortunate, consumers.

Nader's Vision: Its Prospects

What Nader seems to want is a new kind of economic system that would be "broken down into as small parts as are economically possible."[53] His particular concern is to get rid of the large and unyielding bureaucracy that is essential to any large-scale enterprise, public or private. Nader believes that the costs of large-scale production—in terms of the power of the enterprise to be unresponsive to its constituents and to ignore the sense of alienation that comes to people as they work and live in such an atmosphere—outweigh the productive economies of scale.[54] He points to evidence that in many cases production can be as efficient on a smaller scale as on a larger scale. In addition to the smaller scale, he would have the enterprises in the economy "run by the constituency they are supposed to serve."[55] For Nader this means, for example, that retail stores would be run as cooperatives and the people who buy at the store would decide what products and grades of products would be sold. Similarly, he would have production workers take a much greater responsibility for decisions made in manufacturing establishments.[56]

Nader denies that the kind of system he espouses is socialistic. He maintains that under socialism where, to use his words, "the government would own the means of production," there is the same problem with bureaucracy that there is under the private-property system of capitalism. Nader's primary goal is that any economic system provide full and rewarding lives for individual citizens, and he believes this is possible only when individual citizens have real, not token, responsibilities. His system, he claims, would be one of "initiatory" rather than "participatory" democracy as the latter is, in his words, "too passive."[57]

The essential ingredient of Nader's vision of a new economic system is people who will be willing to exchange the benefits of mass consumption that have come with industrial affluence for the opportunity and obligation to direct their own lives. Such an exchange would mean less real output, as the productive system moved toward less specialization and less division of labor. (This is so because whatever may be the gain in people's personal, as opposed to material, lives, an enterprise run as a true cooperative, with participation by all its members, will have a higher cost output than one run more efficiently by specialists.) In line with what Nader calls professional citizenship, people in the new system will have to be willing to give up time formerly spent in their own selfish interests in order to contribute to the smaller enterprises of which they are now an essential part. Nader's position on this point is vividly expressed when he lashes out at "a society which has thousands of full-time manicurists and pastry-makers but less than a dozen citizen-specialists fighting full time" against what he sees as malfeasance on the part of business and government.[58]

It is difficult to see how Nader's idea of competitive markets will operate in this system based on cooperation. The competitive system requires competition among consumers as well as among producers. And in the United States competition serves not only as a philosophical basis for the system of production, it also serves as a philosophical basis for the system of social relationships. Cooperation bypasses the market to provide a different mechanism for both production and social relationships. It is not clear how Nader would move from the break-up of large corporate and government bureaucracies to a system that includes both competition and cooperation.

In the end, however, the success of Nader's program and his hopes for a "just society" does not depend on whether the power of corporate enterprise can be controlled. It depends on the existence of millions of consumers who share Nader's ideals and who would be willing to exchange affluence for responsibility. There is little evidence that idealism exists to such an extent among American consumers. Nader received immense publicity and consumer identification when he first began his work ten years ago. But during the last few years he has received considerably less attention, and it is doubtful if at the present time he can generate the level of individual action that is basic to the long-range changes he sees as the solution to consumer problems.

Advocacy and Education

If the current "consumerism" is to be a more effective force, people are going to have to give more importance to their roles as consumers.

Carol Foreman (October 1974)

Even though in recent years the most conspicuous efforts for the consumer have been identified with Ralph Nader and governmental consumer advocates, the consumer movement has found support from other quarters as well. Several national consumer organizations have been formed. *Consumers Union* and *Consumers' Research* have been joined by other publications and columnists seeking to help consumers in their search for the kinds of information that will give them their "money's worth." The labor movement has identified itself with the consumer's cause and has used its resources and influence in programs for consumer organization, legislation, and information. And finally, there has come to be a renewed interest in the possibilities for additional protection for consumers through formal programs of consumer education.

Consumer Organizations

A continuing goal of the consumer movement has been to establish a large, central organization at the national level. Such an organization would give a needed cohesiveness and coordination for the diverse elements supporting the consumer's cause and provide a national forum to lend weight and prestige to the various groups speaking in the name of the consumer.

The first such organization, begun in 1933 as the Emergency Conference of Consumer Organizations, got as far as setting up headquarters in Washington and starting a biweekly newspaper. It lacked any sort of financial backing, however, and lasted less than a year. Some four years later a second organization was started for the same purpose. The Consumers' National Federation, as it was called, contemplated individual consumer memberships as well as the affiliation of interested groups. The Federation continued for several years without any spectacular results, and it passed out of existence sometime during World War II. (Unlike people, organizations are more heralded at birth than at death.)

With the impetus given the movement by the renewed interest in consumers in the early 1960s, another national organization, the Consumer Federation of America (CFA), was begun in 1967. There are some 200 organizations—labor unions, state and local consumer organizations, credit unions, and rural electric cooperatives—which currently identify themselves with the CFA. The CFA sees its role as an action-oriented one, serving as a clearinghouse on consumer legislation and as a consumer representative appearing at public hearings and bringing pressure for consumer legislation. It is also active in encouraging and supporting grass roots consumer organizations. The CFA has a staff of about ten people and a budget of some 200 thousand dollars.

Currently the CFA is the most prominent consumer-organization voice being heard at Congressional hearings.[1] Its executive director, Carol Foreman, is an energetic and effective lobbyist who describes herself as an "agrarian radical." Under her direction, the CFA garnered the support of many in the 1974 Congress and has spoken out on many issues affecting the consumer interest, including controls on natural gas and petroleum, food price supports, and the proposed agency for consumer protection. Even though the political activism of CFA has done much to publicize the consumer in Washington, the long-run success of CFA will depend on the degree of support from the affiliated organizations and their members. It has, however, had a longer life than any such previous organization.

In addition to CFA at the national level, there are dozens of state and local consumer organizations active across the country.[2] Many of these are the PIRGs and Citizen Action Groups begun by Nader and his associates. Some are an outgrowth of neighborhood-development programs; others are associated with colleges and universities. Many are small, locally organized groups with constantly changing leadership and membership. The effectiveness of these organizations varies over time and from place to place; they are largely dependent on voluntary staffing and their viability is directly related to the prominence of consumer issues. In times of inflation or rising food prices, local organizations attract the interest and support of new members, but this is apt to be temporary and cannot be the basis for sustained development.

Consumer Publications

In contrast to the numerous consumer organizations that have come and gone and in contrast to the ebb and flow of consumer activity over the nearly fifty years since the consumer movement began in 1927, two consumer-information services, Consumers' Research and Consumers Union, have continued without interruption. These two services were organized to provide consumers with impartial information on goods and services on the premise, as Consumers Union states it, that "any economic system based on free choice succeeds only insofar as its citizens are given useful information to choose rationally among competing products and competing services."[3] Though serving the same purpose, the two organizations have played essentially different roles in the consumer movement.

Consumers' Research, since its foundation in 1927, has been run by F.J. Schlink. Schlink has staunchly defended the concept of the independent consumer who, armed with sufficient information and energy, can make the kinds of decisions necessary to assure that he gets "his money's worth." Schlink stood outside the mainstream of the consumer movement in the thirties because he did not believe that government representation of the consumer would achieve any lasting benefits. In his view, government had "sold out to business," and consumers could expect little genuine help there. Schlink still holds this view. Editorializing in 1974 on the increasing activism for government support for the consumer, he wrote, "the alert and informed consumer is his own best friend."[4]

Consumers Union, like Consumers' Research, is engaged in testing consumer goods and services and funds this information service through subscriptions to its monthly publication, *Consumer Reports*. Though in its early days it concentrated on low-cost household items—like food, soap, clothing, and bedding—it now provides information on a wide variety of consumer products—automobiles, sports and hobby equipment, tools, TVs, and phonograph equipment—as well as the more usual items in household use. And, increasingly in recent years, CU has extended its concern to consumer "products" like safe drinking water, health insurance, mass transportation, and banking services. Its readers are primarily college-educated, upper-middle-income families. CU estimates a readership of about two million.

By contrast with Consumers' Research, CU has always seen itself as a part of the consumer movement. Its long-time president, Colston E. Warne, has been a central figure in the consumer movement since the end of the 1930s. CU has been critical of what it considers excessive and misleading advertising on the part of business. It has called for grade labeling and standards for consumer products, for the release of product information gathered by government agencies, and for a "department of consumers." It publicizes rulings made by the FDA and FTC on products and advertising and has consistently criticized government regulatory agencies for neglecting to uphold the consumer's interest. CU currently has a Washington office to foster and promote its consumer advocacy in government.

CU's joint policies of political advocacy and consumer information have caused some conflict within the organization. On the one hand, there are those who maintain that CU should restrict itself to product information based on testing and leave controversial issues alone. They disapprove of CU's interest in public issues such as national health insurance.[5] In this camp are also a number of CU employees whose union, in May 1975, accused CU's management of "squandering money on social activism."[6] On the other hand, there are those who support CU's interest in political activities and are critical of what they see as CU's reluctance to participate in an even wider range of consumer activities. Criticism from this camp reached a peak in the summer of 1975 when Ralph Nader resigned from the Board of Directors of CU, charging that CU should devote more of its "energy and resources . . . toward changing major consumer injustices through consumer action" and should "realize more of its potential in the area of consumer investigation, advocacy and organization."[7]

In responding to these criticisms, CU has generally leaned toward those who favor testing and information over advocacy. In an editorial in early 1975, CU acknowledged the value judgments implicit in any stand on a public issue and stated that in the future it would "label clearly those reports that, on balance, present a viewpoint on a controversial issue rather than buying data on goods and services."[8] In responding to Nader later in the year, Rhoda H. Karpatkin, executive director of CU, recognized the need for greater advocacy but reaffirmed the "impartial product-testing and reporting program" as "CU's unique contribution to the consumer interest."[9] Whatever may be the predilection of CU's Board, it is surely the case that the activities CU elects to pursue are funded by the subscriptions to a magazine based on testing information.

Less closely associated with the consumer movement are a number of other magazines and syndicated columns carrying information and advice about spending and money. *Changing Times* is a monthly magazine published by Kiplinger as a "service for families," much as the Kiplinger newsletter is for businessmen. It covers a broad range of family expenditures including health, education, investment, and leisure. It does not recommend specific brands nor is it oriented toward consumer advocacy. Time Inc. publishes a similar monthly, *Money*. Both of these magazines are geared to the expenditures and life styles of upper-middle-income families. The most widely read newspaper column is that of Sylvia Porter whose daily column *Your Dollar* appears in hundreds of newspapers across the country. Porter's lively discussions combine consumer counsel with lucid explanations of the current economic situation.

Labor's Part in the Consumer Movement

The labor movement was late in coming to espouse the consumer's cause. During the thirties when the consumer movement had its initial growth, labor was preoccupied with securing its own position and could not afford to advocate any other special interests.[a] Nor was it always evident to labor that workers' goals were in harmony with consumers' goals. Increasingly, however, after World

---

[a]That CU grew out of a split with Consumers' Research on the issue of union membership did serve to tie labor to one element of the consumer movement. At the same time, F.J. Schlink's hostility to labor did not enhance the relationship between labor and consumer.

War II as labor became more secure in its economic position, it came to see the consumer movement's goal of more efficient consumer spending as consistent with labor's own goal of greater worker income. Labor now identifies workers as consumers, and organized labor as part of the consumer movement. In 1973, for example, the AFL-CIO Convention called for a "consumer protection agency, improved product warranties and no fault insurance." It asserted that "millions of consumers are defrauded in the market place every year when they are sold shoddy products and unsafe food."[10]

In labor's view, organization is a key to power. To this end, labor not only urges its local labor organizations to participate in consumer activities but also has promoted consumer organization at the national level. The AFL-CIO sponsored the 1966 Washington Consumer Assembly which was the impetus for the Consumer Federation of America. A number of unions were charter members of this organization and have been a significant source of support.

In its program for strengthening the position of consumers, labor also has relied heavily on legislation. It sees legislation and government regulation as "the major screen" for consumer protection against unsafe and poor-quality products. Labor has consistently backed consumer legislation—the truth in lending and truth in packaging bills, auto safety, meat inspection, and the establishment of a consumer-protection agency. One spokeman has asserted that "unions have been the single most influential force on both national and state levels in securing most of what legislative gains [have been] made on behalf of consumers."[11]

In addition to organization and legislation, the labor movement has made some efforts to promote consumer education, particularly at the local level. This program has been based on the proposition that without effective consumer education for workers, "the gains made at the bargaining tables are lost across the counters." Consumer education has tended to concentrate on specific problems such as credit, health insurance, and legal assistance and protection. There is also emphasis on avoiding fraud in door-to-door sales and useless and quack drugs. The monthly AFL-CIO publication, *The American Federationist*, carries a consumer column by Sidney Margolis which discusses the specific ways consumers can make dollars go farther. In recent years, however, there appears to be less organized-union support for consumer education.

Several explanations can be given for labor's efforts to promote the consumer interest. Labor's own explanation, of course, is that consumer protection becomes another, and necessary, service of unions to their members. A second explanation for labor's interest in consumers is that labor can in this way identify not just with workers but with all Americans who are consumers. Thus labor projects itself not as a special-interest group seeking the worker's advantages at the expense of others but as an ally of all consumers. Labor, like Congress, comes to support the consumer who is the "unrepresented man in our society."

Labor can profitably espouse the consumer's cause when consumers' interests complement rather than compete with labor's own interests. The consumer's interest in low prices and high quality, in more product information and in consumer representation does not threaten labor's interest in higher incomes and greater job security. Much consumer legislation affects producers rather than workers—truth in packaging and lending, meat inspection, and the various health and safety measures. Labor can urge this kind of consumer legislation without fear of hurting workers as producers of income. And there are cases where the consumer's interest coincides with labor's. In the discussion of grain sales to Russia, for example, labor could oppose increased deliveries (in Russian ships) on the basis of higher consumer prices rather than on the basis of lost worker income. Finally, if there is any advantage to unions to emphasize the old conflicts between labor and management, a consumer program works for the former as a consumer and against the latter as a producer.

When, however, there is a conflict between the interests of workers and consumers, labor has to look to its own defenses and to assert its own interests over and beyond those of the consumer. In the bargaining to get a passable consumer-representation bill, labor managed to get labor matters exempt from any review by the new consumer-protection agency. Such review could, of course, be damaging to labor as the consumer's interest in wage settlements, restrictive labor policies, strikes, and import duties and quotas would be different from that of labor. The militancy of public employees for higher wages is a good case in point here. In a similar conflict of interests, the Sheetworkers Union, which was a charter member of the Consumer Federation of America, opposed CFA's position in favor of the prohibition of throw-away cans.[12]

The prolonged economic downturn of the 1970s, the prospect of increased competition from foreign production, and the drive to protect the environment seem to have undermined the ties between labor's interest and the consumer's interest. Increasingly, labor's interest in jobs runs counter to the consumer's interest in lower prices. At the same time the growing political appeal of the consumer movement makes identification with it a source of strength for labor.[13] The basic issues between labor and the consumer movement, however, remain "unformulated," and it is too soon to predict what will be the long-term relationship between the two.[14] Likewise, in its search for support, the consumer movement necessarily counts on organized labor and cites "the new visibility of the consumer movement" as the carrot for labor's "forthcoming" support.[15]

Consumer Education in the Thirties

Consumer advocates have consistently viewed consumer education as an integral part of the work of the consumer movement. They have urged the adoption of consumer education as lifetime training—in school and college, as well as in adult and continuing education. In particular, consumer education has been held out as a way of ameliorating poverty among minority groups and the elderly. Within the movement, education has had the dual role of providing to consumers the information they need to be efficient in the marketplace and of creating among consumers the kind of awareness that would lead to support for political action on behalf of consumers. The consumer movement envisioned education as the primary vehicle by which it would seek to promote efficient consumers and effective consumer political pressure. Education came to outweigh other efforts that could have concentrated on establishing consumer organizations, on consumer action through strikes or boycotts, or pushing for government legislation or representation. The consumer movement has seen education in the community as well as in formal schooling as an efficient and noncontroversial way to achieve consumer efficiency and awareness.

This concentration on education came about partly because other efforts of the consumer movement were less successful. After the mid-thirties, as chances faded for accomplishing very much for the consumer through legislation and representation, the hopes for educating consumers grew brighter. It is hard to find any other similar movement—not even the cooperative movement—that has put so much emphasis on the process of education as a means to gain strength.

The early consumer movement conceived of consumer education in a very broad sense. Consumer education was not to be limited to providing consumers with information about buying but was to give people the background necessary to see and understand the whole role of the consumer in society. The concept of consumer education originally included a wide range of activities, as much *outside* formal education as within, by which people "of all ages" could be made to realize and act on their rights and responsibilities as consumers. But in particular, the movement wanted definite programs to provide various groups with specifically designed material in consumer education. These programs were to include the teaching of specially prepared material with specially trained instructors in elementary schools, high schools, and colleges, either in specific courses in consumer training or along with other courses in the curriculum. The movement sought also to extend the programs as far as possible to other groups in the community which would, or were felt should, be reached with information about how to become better consumers.

As general interest in consumer education grew during the 1930s, organizations developed committed to promote consumer education as a whole. The most significant of these was the Stephens College Institute for Consumer Education, established in 1937 at Stephens College (Columbia, Missouri) by a 250 thousand dollar grant from the Sloan Foundation. One of the major contributions of the Institute was a yearly National Conference on Consumer Education. Groups of as many as 400 or 500 gathered to attend lectures and participate in workshops devoted to increasing the quantity, and to improving the quality, of consumer education.[16] The concern of the Institute was to provide consumer education not only within the framework of school and college but in the larger community as well. The life of the Institute coincided with the early years of success for the consumer movement, and in no small way contributed to its strength.

Other groups also took up the cause of consumer education. In the spring of 1939, the Consumer Education Association was formed for teachers with this special interest. Within a few years, the Association had a membership of more than 700 and was able to hold two annual meetings. The American Home Economics Association established a Consumer Education Service that distributed a newsletter with information of particular interest to home economists working in consumer education. The American Association of University Women considered the consumer's interest a part of its basic program and published consumer-education materials for use by its local groups.

Most important, however, for consumer education was the support of the public schools. By 1941, it was estimated that some 5 to 10 percent of American high schools were offering special courses in consumer economics and that many more schools were providing consumer-education material in business, social studies, and home economics courses. The Educational Policies Commission of the National Education Association in its *Purposes of Education in American Democracy* pointed out the importance of consumer education. Several years later the National Association of Secondary School Principals (a department of the NEA) set up curriculum guides for teaching consumer education. The consumer movement asserted that "the educational expansion of the past decade has witnessed no movement that has gained greater momentum than has Consumer Education."[17]

But the consumer movement's hopes for education were not fulfilled. The women's groups lost interest. More significantly, following World War II consumer education in the schools became entangled in the conflict between the consumer's interest and the viewpoint of business. The same kind of distrust and animosity that flared up in other parts of the consumer movement found its way into consumer education. Public education could not be insensitive to the fears of business, with the result that consumer education was considerably watered down from what the consumer movement expected it to be. The schools suggested that learning such things as "shrewdness in bargaining" and "the protection of one's own interests against exploiters, etc." might lead to "cynicism and a calculating 'me first' attitude."[18] The public schools could not handle the conflict between consumers and producers that is implicit in economic theory. Even though consumer education did not disappear from school curricula during the fifties, what was left did little to promote the consumer's cause.

Consumer Education in the Seventies

The consumer-education programs that have come with the revived consumer interest of the past decade are considerably more narrow than the consumer-education programs of the thirties. The earlier efforts for widespread consumer education were essentially an extension of the consumer movement, a means by which the consumer movement sought not only to help the consumer assume his "rightful" place in the economy but also to expand its influence and create effective consumer political pressure. By contrast, consumer education today is not so much a vehicle for the expansion of the consumer movement as it is the means to arm buyers for the confrontation with sellers. At the same time consumer education today, like forty years ago, is seen as a combination of providing straight information about price and quality and the knowledge and understanding necessary to be an effective consumer in the modern complex economy.

If the focus of consumer education is more narrow than before, it has achieved a wider group of advocates who have great faith in the ability of consumer education to help the consumer protect his position in the market. In addition to the traditional support shown by consumer groups and the public schools, there is support from Presidential consumer appointments, the labor movement, and, in recent years, from Congress in the form of funds for consumer education to the Office of Education in the Department of Health, Education, and Welfare. Business has also joined the ranks of supporters to espouse consumer education as a "vehicle for preventing future consumer unrest."[19]

The Presidential consumer assistants have advocated greater efforts for consumer education in the schools and among target groups of the population. Under Mrs. Peterson's leadership, several national conferences were held focusing on ways of implementing consumer education in the public school curriculum. In his 1971 message on consumers to Congress, President Nixon asserted that "consumer education is an integral part of consumer protection. It is vital if the consumer is to make wise judgments in the marketplace." Under Mrs. Knauer the Office of Consumer Affairs has developed several sets of materials to be used in consumer-education programs for adults and children, as well as for minority groups like the Indian, the elderly, or other low-income people. The Office of Consumer Affairs has also sought to make available to consumers some of the immense amounts of government information that may be of interest and help to consumers. Twice a month it publishes a *Consumer News* sheet that gives information about consumer-related actions and activities of the various agencies of the federal government. It also makes available a guide to Federal Consumer Services. Through the Consumer Information Center of the General Services Administration, Mrs. Knauer, as the President's Special Assistant for Consumer Affairs, issues a quarterly pamphlet, "Consumer Information," which is a compilation of federal publications that may be useful to consumers.

Congress has also expressed its interest in and support for consumer education. In 1968, it first authorized federal funds to states for "consumer and homemaking" education through the Office of Education in HEW. Four years later Congress authorized the appointment of a "Director of Consumer Education" in the Office of Education and the preparation of curriculum materials that would "prepare consumers for participation in the marketplace." In 1974 it went one step further to direct HEW to set up an "Office of Consumer Education" to be responsible for preparing curriculum and curriculum materials and to award grants directed toward community education, workshops, and training. The Office of Consumer Education issued preliminary guidelines for these activities in the fall of 1975.

It is on the premise that consumer education for young people can be most readily and easily provided through the public school system that Presidential consumer advisors, and consumer groups in general, have continued to urge public schools to offer more in the way of consumer education. The educational system on the whole, however, has been slow to respond. Consumer education comes largely through home economics and business courses. Because there is no "standard" consumer education course, the materials are usually produced by local school districts and are heavily dependent on material from business sources. Even though the National Education Association has never repudiated consumer education, the Consumer Education Study material, for example, which was prepared between 1945 and 1955 has not been revised, and nothing has been substituted for it.

The rising interest in consumer affairs does seem to have moved some leaders in public education to revive programs in consumer education. The State Education Department of New York has developed a series of materials to be used in consumer education. The CU Consumer Educational Materials Project, set up under a grant from the Office of Education, offers a wide variety of techniques for dealing with consumer education for different age groups.[20] The Joint Council of Economic Education, in line with its goal of increased economic literacy, lists a wide number of district-wide and individual classroom units currently underway in various sections of the country. And the legislatures of several states, including Illinois, Oregon, and Wisconsin, have mandated consumer education in all public schools.

It is interesting to note that the fortunes of consumer education in the public schools have depended less on pressures arising through the consumer movement than on currents within the educational system itself. In the 1930s, consumer education coincided with the emphasis in education on "education for life" and "education for living." This was the idea that schools had the primary responsibility for training young people to find useful and satisfying roles in society. The suitability of a subject in the schools was measured by its "social utility or actual use in the 'real business of living.' "[21] Then, with the Sputnik events of the 1950s, education was criticized for its overemphasis on "practical" subjects and with the return to greater stress on traditional academic subjects consumer education lost much of its appeal to educators. Twenty years later, however, in response to the educational cry of "relevance," consumer education has again found a place in the public schools. Cheering that it is in the limelight again, CU asserts that consumer education offers "great potential as a vehicle for reforming education in the U.S."[22]

Conflicts in Consumer Education

In general, the focus of consumer education has been in two areas. In one direction, it has emphasized the necessity for consumer information—about goods and services, about budgeting and credit, about fraud and deception—as a tool for bringing about increased consumer satisfaction. In another direction, consumer education has been built around the economic role of the consumer. Here the emphasis is on competitive theory, decision-making in the market, and the role of the consumer and consumption from the perspective of the economy as a whole.

In the first area, programs are necessarily limited to a "how-to" approach and are heavily weighted with descriptive material about how consumers do and should behave. Categories of expenditures are listed with sources of information about each. The assumption is that consumers should, and can, gain expertise in all areas of expenditures. The result is that the materials emphasize the work in shopping rather than the reward in the goods bought. Effort is made to avoid the appearance of "siding" with consumers against legitimate (as opposed to "unscrupulous") business. The materials are almost all uniformly dull and uninteresting.

In the second direction, consumer education tends to become *economics* rather than *consumer economics*. ("Consumer economics" has never gained much authority among academic economists.) Only by analyzing the competitive model—and the divergence from it of monopoly and corporate power—can this type of program focus on the consumer. And even here the consumer is not one of "flesh and blood" but one who is rational and utility-maximizing. Because economics takes wants as *given*, economists have not dealt with the question of basic consumer needs and how these might relate to the total economic system. Most importantly, these courses are taught by economists, and economists, given the whole range of economic problems that need to be dealt with, are not particularly interested in dealing with consumer problems as such. If consumer economics has been a stepchild of economics, it is also important to note that it has not been able to achieve an independent status outside of academic economics.

A continuing problem for consumer education in schools and other publicly funded agencies has been: What position should it take between the producer interest of business and the consumer interest in lower price and greater quantity? In urging consumer efficiency in the market, consumer education has to support the buyer's interest against that of the seller. Such a stance is often interpreted as a direct and unwarranted attack on business. As a consequence, business often sees public efforts at consumer education as unfair to business. In matters of advertising, packaging, and consumer action as opposed to producer action, publicly supported consumer education has seldom taken a firm stand.

In particular, this question of point of view has been a problem in the development of consumer education for low-income groups. These groups are usually less educated, less informed, and less mobile than higher-income groups. They also seem more susceptible to the pressures of advertising and salesmanship in what David Caplovitz calls "compensatory consumption." Here, says Caplovitz, "appliances, automobiles and the dream of a home of their own can become compensations for the blocked social mobility."[23] Such consumers are more open than others to abuses from unscrupulous salesmen and lenders. Yet efforts to help these consumers to learn more rational patterns of spending is necessarily contrary to the interests of the businesses with which they deal. As a consequence, business often questions the legitimacy of government efforts at consumer education. For example, in 1966 *Nation's Business* called information from cooperatives and the consumer testing services "questionable weapons" in the "escalating consumer education phase of government's war on poverty."

In spite of the basic issues that divide business and consumers, business has consistently been in the position of supporting the idea of consumer education. The main reason for this is that business has found education to be a useful alternative to increased government protection of consumers. When consumer advocates call for further consumer legislation or consumer representation in government, business can advance consumer education as a means to an "informed and effective consumer directing the free enterprise economy." In the make-believe context of rational and informed individuals buying in competitive markets, consumer education is neither controversial nor a threat to the status quo.

The continuing frustration for consumer educators has not been so much a lack of support as it has been a lack of well-defined goals and methods. This inability to focus clearly on what *is* consumer education can best be understood in terms of the disparity between a very broadly defined set of purposes and the rather narrow set of concepts out of which consumer education must be taught. As a consequence of this divergence between task and tools, consumer education has been handicapped by an absence of sense of purpose and an ambivalence of viewpoint.

Two current definitions of consumer education suggest the almost limitless task assigned consumer education.

Consumer education seeks to provide consumers with the information and skills they need to deal effectively with the institutions, agencies, corporations, social conditions, and economic and ecological problems that affect them daily.
Education Division of Consumers Union, 1973

Consumer education should help each person understand his own value system; develop a sound decision-making procedure in the marketplace based upon his values; evaluate alternatives in the marketplace, and get the best buy for his money; understand his rights and responsibilities as a consumer and as a member of society; and fulfill his role in directing a free-enterprise system."

United States Office of Consumer Affairs, 1973

In both these statements consumer education is so broadly defined that it encompasses nearly every aspect of a person's life in a highly industrialized and monetized society. Consumer education is to provide people—young and old— with the knowledge of how to cope with "institutions, agencies, corporations, social conditions, and economic and ecological problems that affect them daily." To accomplish this, consumer education has to teach values clarification, decision-making, and economic theory, and provide an almost infinite amount of information—both private and government—about the wide variety of increasingly complex goods and services available to consumers and about the administrative procedures for intervention if consumer rights are abused. Then consumer education holds out the promise that if a person thus is informed and knowledgeable, he will be a sovereign consumer who can "fulfill his role in directing a free-enterprise system."

In contrast to education for life which consumer education sets as its goal, the theoretical concepts that consumer education can draw on are narrowly prescribed by the economic analysis of the consumer/buyer operating in competitive (or what should be competitive) markets. However broadly consumer goals may be defined, the theoretical model from which any analysis of consumers must proceed is that of conventional economic theory. In this model, wants and choices are a *given*, decision-making is defined in terms of the rational human being weighing prices of alternate goods, and consumer goals are a sterile concept of getting the most goods and services for the least expenditure. Most importantly, economic theory has no way at all, beyond the still unsatisfactory analysis of monopolistic competition and oligopoly, to deal with the social complexities of "institutions, agencies, corporations, social conditions, and economic and ecological problems" that make up the daily lives of most American consumers.

Advocates of consumer education hold out the promise that understanding is the solution to consumer problems. But when that understanding is bound within the narrow framework of conventional economic theory, it is little wonder that there has been a wide difference between promise and reward. Given this situation, there has been little consensus on what programs in consumer education should include. As a result, practitioners of consumer education have difficulty in setting their objectives and in evaluating the usefulness of any programs that are carried out.

As it is currently conceived, consumer education should be worthwhile because it contributes in some way to consumer satisfaction or well-being—either through an increase in the quantity of goods and services consumed or through an increase in disposable income by way of lower prices and better goods. That consumers in general do not appear to be interested in consumer education and are not anxious to "study" in order to realize these benefits has led some economists to question the purposes and goals of consumer economics. D.I. Padberg argues that with increasing real incomes most people are no longer forced to watch every dollar of expenditure.[24] What he calls "survival shopping" is to most people less important than it used to be. He maintains that people are caught between their increasingly humanitarian interests and the "frugality" that has been "lauded and honored" as the traditional "survival and subsistence" consumer value. In a similar vein, Gerhard Scherf points out that current consumer education concentrates on enabling consumers to get more goods and services as a means of alleviating dissatisfaction.[25] He asserts, however, that higher incomes do not appear to bring greater consumer satisfaction and argues the need for education that will bring consumers an "increase in their level of life satisfaction." Scherf notes the work done to increase job satisfaction through involvement in decision-making and understanding. He calls for similar work in consumer education to emphasize interpersonal goal-orientation rather than the individual means-orientation of conventional consumer education.

These may be harbingers of coming changes. But to date consumer education has not made any significant impact on the lives of most consumers and has never made the hoped for contribution to the consumer movement. It has not created informed consumers who, through wise buying decisions, can direct the development of the economy. Nor has it created large groups of politically conscious consumers who see the necessity of bringing consumer pressure to bear on governments. Perhaps no program of consumer education can achieve these ends, but without real changes in its goals and methods, the increased interests in consumer education are likely to come to naught.

7

Pretenders to the Throne

[I] t is absurd to maintain that the private enterprise system is directed towards supplying consumers' needs. Rather, consumers are the pasture on which enterprise feeds. We are used to a system that is run for the benefit of producers, in which the advantage to consumers is merely incidental . . ..

Joan Robinson
(Economics: An Awkward Corner)

Many aspects of the consumer movement have changed during the forty years or so since its beginnings. The earlier movement found its vehicle in consumer representatives and consumer educators and in women's organizations; its impetus today comes principally from consumer activitists and from within government and organized labor. In contrast to an earlier time when there was an almost religious fervor about "sovereign consumers in competitive markets," there is little rhetoric about such a proposition today. But the analysis within which the consumer movement is defined—its theoretical framework—has remained the same. It is not, as some contend,[1] that the theory of the consumer movement is undeveloped, but rather that its theoretical framework continues to be that of conventional economic theory. Today, as in its beginnings, the consumer movement continues to define its objectives in terms of fully informed consumers buying goods in competitive markets from producers who have no market power. This definition, more than anything else, explains the consumer movement's limited and sporadic activities and the unpromising prospects for its accomplishing any real change in the consumer's position in the economy. The purpose of this chapter is to show how the consumer movement's reliance on classical economic theory has thwarted the achievement of its objectives and weakened its appeal for a constituency. The final chapter will then suggest, on the basis of this analysis, some possible directions consumer activity may take in the future.

The Consequences of Classical Theory

From its beginnings in the early 1930s to the present, the consumer movement has been bound by economic theory's analysis of consumers. The reason for this is quite simple: *consumer* has meaning only in economic terms. Consumers are

83

not voters, citizens, or even community members; consumers are individual human beings who use goods and services for their own purposes. In market-oriented economies like that of the United States, the accepted economic definition holds that consumers function in markets where private firms produce and sell, and consumers buy and use. By this definition such markets can work effectively—i.e., so that neither producers nor consumers are at a disadvantage—only when producers are competitive and consumers are fully informed about all the possible choices and prices of goods and services. In this theoretical framework consumers have power; they are sovereign; their interests are protected from abuse by producers.

Such a framework is, of course, the basis for a laissez-faire policy toward the economy. Consumers know their own personal values and goals and are free to act on them as they purchase goods and services. Any government edicts on what consumers should buy would violate the exercise of consumer choice. Similarly, if competition among producers assures the product consumers want at the lowest price and prohibits the exercise of market power, then there is no reason for government intervention. Only when consumers are not informed or are misinformed or when markets are not competitive is there recourse to government for consumer "protection."

This theoretical framework also serves to distinguish between the consumer's interest and the public interest. The consumer's interest is in getting the most and best goods for the lowest price. This is in opposition to the producer's interest which is in increasing profits through higher prices, lower costs and greater volume. The public interest lies in a balancing of these two interests. Consumer goals and producer goals are necessarily conflicting, and only as long as competition prevails will market forces work out the best possible solution for both.

Within this theoretical framework, efforts for the consumer have mainly focused on reinforcing or protecting the bargaining position of the consumer in the market. The consumer movement's endeavors for objective information such as "truth in packaging" and "truth in lending," its criticism of advertising, its urging for government action to foster competition within the economy, and its insistence on the need for consumer representation in government to compensate for the lack of competition have all centered around the goal of establishing the necessary conditions for a competitive market system and thus of helping the consumer to "fulfill his role in directing a free-enterprise system."[2]

In accepting such a goal, the consumer movement does not seem to have questioned whether the theory on which it is based is useful for its objectives. It does not seem to have considered whether the promotion of rationality in consumers and competition in markets is useful for understanding and promoting the role of an essentially nonrational consumer in a noncompetitive economy. By depending on such a theory to define the consumer's position in the economy, the consumer movement has been bound to positions that handicap it in dealing with modern American consumption. In having to take the rational consumer with a given set of choices operating in competitive markets, the efforts for consumer organization have accomplished little, and the work for consumers in other areas has not basically changed or strengthened the consumer's position in the economy. (This does not mean that there is a ready substitute, a point which will be discussed later.)

To analyze the limitations of economic theory for the consumer movement, we can consider the following four issues or concerns, which have been central to the work of the consumer movement: (1) the basis of the appeal of the consumer movement to its constituency, (2) the question of what goods consumers want to buy and the related question of how most efficiently to buy them, (3) the consumer movement's conflict with business, and (4) the question of how new areas of economic analysis, especially macroeconomic theory and consumer-behavior studies, relate to the modern consumer. It can be shown that in each of these areas the consumer movement has been thwarted by its dependence on classical economic theory.

In its appeal to a potential constituency, the consumer movement has been bound by an economic analysis that emphasizes characteristics that are unattractive to most Americans. The consumer movement has had to work within a theory that portrays the consumer as a budget-minded, rational individual, relentlessly pushing toward maximizing his satisfaction. Such a consumer has to think well ahead, to "wait" before buying, to consider the usefulness and serviceability of a good as its most important characteristic. The consumer defined by the theory watches every penny. To get the best value and achieve maximum satisfaction, the consumer needs always to be weighing small expenditures against small gains.

There is a conflict between the image people have of a *consumer* and the image they have of *real* people. The consumer movement has emphasized low price and high quality in a society that honors the ability to spend lavishly. The movement has stressed the notion of *economizing* when much of the thrust of national sentiment has been toward exuberant spending. The consumer movement has dramatized highly advertised foods, "hidden" credit costs, and deceptive packaging the correction of which would mean only small savings for a single family; thus people tend to associate the consumer movement with a kind of miserly, "penny-pinching" attitude. This attitude, however much it may contribute to the efficiency of consumers in competitive markets, is not highly regarded as a personal trait in American society. While Americans may not place as high a value on conspicuous consumption as they did when Veblen invented the phrase seventy-five years ago, they still accord high status to those who can buy the higher-priced of two similar goods. At the same time, by stressing the thought and effort needed for wise consumption, the consumer movement has put consumption on a par with toil rather than with production. Working may be tedious and hard, but it brings status and income. But being a "wise" consumer contributes relatively little to income and even less to status. The consumer movement is still preoccupied with values of self-denial and frugality in a society where such values have little pay-off.

The consumer movement has also emphasized the need for consumers to be well-informed about the goods and services they purchase. They not only need to know where they can get a good at the lowest price, but they also need to make decisions about quality, usefulness, safety, durability, and cost of operation and repair. But with the surfeit of information that is available and with the increasing variety and sophistication of consumer goods, this information is costly. Learning to sort out and understand the particular information that is needed for a purchase involves an expenditure of time and effort that many people are unwilling to make.[3] People do not want to spend time doing research on a proposed purchase, or even ask useful questions of a salesperson. People have "better" or "other" things to do with their time, which is simply another way of saying that, whatever the gains to be achieved by deliberation prior to purchase, they are not worth the cost in time and effort.

Furthermore, it may be the case that people do not want to analyze their motives for spending or have to justify a particular expenditure. Lack of widespread public clamor for "truth in lending," for example, suggests that people do not relish knowing how much credit actually costs them. In spite of the almost universal use of credit in this country, the Puritan disapproval of borrowing for present consumption hangs on. And even though economists have recognized the trade-off that consumers may (rationally) make between the cost of information and the cost of a good, the consumer movement continues to stress the development of information about goods rather than the goods themselves as the prime source of consumer satisfaction and well-being.

The consumer movement has tried to attract a constituency on a basis that does not appeal to most Americans. Thus, in spite of the fact that "everyone is a consumer," relatively few people have been willing to identify themselves with consumer issues—to join a group, to participate in consumer-education activities, or to provide financial support to consumer organizations. In the minds of most Americans, the concept of consumer projects neither strength nor individuality, nor even likeableness. People do not ordinarily think of themselves as consumers. Nor are they encouraged by others to do so. Business does not use the term in its advertising. The term is restricted almost exclusively to use in economics, within market research, and among sober and purposeful advocates of consumer welfare. In 1940, Stacy May could comment that the work of the consumer movement seemed to be "haunted by a malign influence that leads people, when talking about consumer matters, to speak in terms that are irrefutably noble but overwhelmingly dull."[4] Time has done little to change this. Thirty years later a businessman was quoted as saying, "If you want to be amused for a few hours, it is all right to meet with . . . consumer groups, but I have never known an important idea to come out of these meetings."[5]

The second issue that has been clouded by the dependency of the consumer movement on economic theory is the question of consumer choice—of what goods consumers choose to buy. This is a basic question for consumers and therefore should be of paramount interest to the consumer movement. But in economics the question of what particular goods a consumer chooses is a *given*, and it is, therefore, not a matter for analysis. The economic theory of consumer behavior (indeed, economic theory as a whole) does not allow for any discussion of goals or ends. To do so would be to make value judgments that, in the accepted tenets of the social sciences, are unacceptable. Thus, in spite of the fact that nearly all agree that in consumer education and in other consumer areas people should be helped "to understand their own value systems," nothing can be said in terms of "right" or "wrong" or "good" or "bad" about a consumer's values and his choice of goods.

What the theory of consumer behavior says about choice is that each consumer possesses a given set of wants or preferences that is independent of those of other consumers. What set of goods the consumer actually purchases is that set which, out of a given income and with the prices prevailing in the market, goes the farthest toward fulfilling the wants of the given consumer. All the theory says is that, given the preferences of each consumer and the principle of diminishing marginal utility, what the consumer buys is determined by his income and the prices of goods in the market. According to the theory, the consumer's *buying* pattern changes only in response to changes in income or prices. Nothing is said about how the consumer's basic choices are determined, or changed. Since the theory assumes that consumers act in such a way to maximize utility, then the goods they buy must be the ones they want.

Economists from Marshall on have consistently recognized the shortcomings of such an abstract formulation of consumer choices but, in the pursuit of an objective theory, have had to ignore them. And because of the stricture against value judgments, nothing could be said about the quality of a consumer's wants. Whatever goods the consumer chose, in the theory of consumer demand, became the *given*. There is no way to measure a spending pattern in terms of "better" or "worse."

There is also the question of how the consumer can most efficiently achieve his goals. The theory of consumer demand defines the consumer's goals only in terms of a nonmeasurable unit, utility. By dividing his income among different purchases in such a way as to have the marginal satisfaction of each purchase proportional to its price, the consumer achieves maximum satisfaction. While this analysis is an integral part of the theory of value, it is not very helpful to the consumer movement. In it there is little specific advice for consumers about how to achieve consumption goals. The consumer movement could and did stress the importance of price versus usefulness or utility as a workable version of marginal utility proportional to prices. This, however, degenerated into a kind of "economizing."[a] And, while "economizing" to achieve higher consumption was consistent with both economic analysis and the spirit of the times during the Depression and into World War II, it seems alien to present-day America.

Consequently, even though the consumer's wants and pattern of spending have been of intense interest in the analysis of consumption, the consumer movement has lacked any sort of analytical basis for its efforts to help consumers by "improving" consumption. Suggestions, for instance, that the same goals could be gained by using a less expensive product in place of a more expensive (and often highly advertized) product are seen by business as a threat to its own marketing efforts. They are then condemned on the basis that the consumer movement is interfering with independent consumer choices by meddling with the consumer's pattern of spending. This point is nicely illustrated by the criticism that was made of a worker in consumer education who would "step beyond simply giving poor people advice on how to draw up a family budget and tell them to avoid buying one brand because it costs more than another."[6]

This limitation in the matter of choice-making has been particularly crippling to consumer education which sees its primary task as helping consumers to reach higher consumption levels. Consumer education has been forced into vague generalities about "choosing a goal and working toward it" or into the specifics of "buymanship" and how to economize in consumption. The increasing number of budget studies have provided a sort of average against which consumers could compare their own expenditures, but little has been done to set up or promulgate "ideal" consumption patterns or to suggest other means to consumer satisfaction.

Furthermore, because the consumer movement has had to deal with consumer choice as expressed through the market—i.e., through the goods and services bought individually for their own use—it has been unable to deal with social goods and social costs external to the market. The analysis of these issues is theoretically complex,[7] but the main point is that they are not satisfactorily subject to market determination and must be decided on the basis of voting or some other form of social determination. This means that when consumer advocates take a stand, either for or against a particular form of social consumption, they appear to be partisans in an issue that is a public issue rather than a consumer issue.[b] For this reason, the consumer movement has been unable to pose the question of consumer choice between more private goods and more public goods and has thus cut itself off from effective consideration of public expenditures, which today amount to nearly one third of total expenditures. Similarly, the consumer movement has been limited in its authority to deal with matters of the

---

[a]*Consumer Reports,* for example, suggests in mail solicitation it can help its subscribers save 100 dollars a year. But a consumer might reasonably question whether a 100-dollar saving is worth the time and effort involved in reading twelve issues to find the advice on buying items that will save this amount.

[b]Compare the case of CU and national health insurance discussed in Chapter 6.

environment and the social costs of economic growth in a society increasingly concerned with such problems.

A third problem for the consumer movement that has its roots in economic theory is the consumer movement's conflict with business. The question at issue between the consumer movement and business is whether the consumer is sovereign. The consumer movement maintains that until the consumer is truly sovereign, the economy cannot be operating at an optimum. The consumer movement, therefore, calls for changes in business practices and particularly for federal legislation that will protect the consumer's position in the marketplace. Business, on the other hand, insists that the consumer is sovereign and that nothing further needs to be done to protect him.

[The American businessman] faces as he has always faced the cold, hard measure of the marketplace, the challenge of competition and the harsh judgment of a consumer public quick to exert its own free choice. . . .We built a successful economy . . . on the philosophy that says consumer is king . . . "[8]

Business insists that "the competitive process . . . lies at the very heart of the system under which our nation thrives,"[9] and that attempts by government to interfere with either business or consumers threaten not only consumer choice and business efficiency, but also the system as a whole.

Part of the problem here is that American business is suspicious and critical of the underlying premise of the consumer movement, which is that there is an antagonism or opposition of interests between business and consumers. This premise is based on the fact that in a competitive system consumers are on one side of the market and producers and businesses are on the other. In such a system, gains on one side are losses to the other. The consumer movement takes the stand that the tension between consumers and businesses is real, and part of the system, and that attempts to subvert it are detrimental to the welfare of consumers. Business, however, seeks to mask the conflict and sees consumer advocacy as antibusiness and even anti-American.[c]

The consumer movement's advocacy of legislation to protect the consumer's interest is seen by business as a threat to consumers and to choice. To this end, an advertisement showing a mock list of thirty New York movies theatres all billing exactly the same film suggests that consumer advocates believe there is "too much choice in the marketplace."[10] The advertisement asserts that freedom of choice is the reason why consumers can have "so many good things to choose from" and implies that any efforts toward government-set standards are a move toward dull uniformity and a usurpation of consumer rights. In the same

---

[c]To this end, business has come to rely on the "marketing concept" which holds that legitimate and profitable business activity benefits both producers and consumers. If producers do not put on the market the kinds of goods consumers want, then those producers will not prosper.

way, legislation to establish a federal consumer protection agency is seen as setting up a "consumer czar" who, rather than consumers, would have power to decide what kinds of goods and services consumers should have.[11] Safety regulations are seen by business as costly and detrimental to sales, as in the case of the requirement of interlocking automobile seat belts. Another critic has suggested that consumer legislation is advanced by people "who apparently dislike the entire idea of consumption."[12,d]

The consumer movement has also come into conflict with business because the accepted theory of consumer behavior binds the consumer movement to the market price as the "informational link"[13] between producer and consumer. In the world of economic theory, the market transforms the varied wishes of individual consumers into the impersonal information of price, which serves to tell producers what consumers want or do not want. But, unhappily for the theory, the conditions prevailing in the modern economy have undermined this information link. Because "large-scale production requires prior judgments upon . . . consumer demand,"[14] and because the consumer himself does "not know precisely what he wants" and is "inarticulate" and "irrational in nature," there has been a "progressive weakening of [the price system as] the informational link between producer and consumer."[15] Producers can no longer rely on the market for information about consumer wants. Yet the exigencies of modern industry are such that firms must plan for sales in advance of production. The requirements of large-scale industrial production and their far-reaching significance for the modern American economy is a central theme of John Kenneth Galbraith's *The New Industrial State.* The consumer movement, however, has failed to see that under the new conditions, its criticism of advertising and other business attempts to mold demand represents a direct threat to business's efforts to plan for orderly and profitable production.

There is also conflict with business because of the traditional American affirmation of progress and change which stresses work and free enterprise as the basis of "the American way of life." To criticize business is tantamount to criticizing America. The consumer movement's challenge that the marketplace does not operate fairly appears to business to belittle the claims of the business community that it provides the substance for the world's highest national living standard.

Admittedly, there are some things wrong in the marketplace. But the attacks seem all out of proportion to the wrongs. I am . . . fed to the eyeballs with the

---

dIt is interesting to note, however, that the consumer movement has never become associated with the disposition of parts of the intellectual community to deplore American preoccupation with goods and the mass culture that these goods represent. For this position, see, for example, Russell Lynes, *The Tastemakers* (1954) or Marya Mannes, *But Will It Sell?* (1964).

tolerance that our society shows to its critics. . . . Never in the history of men has society offered so much to so many. . . . The profit motive has led to innovation, [and] greater efficiency.[16]

Yet in their mutual criticism both business and the consumer movement base their positions on the economic doctrine of sovereign consumers in competitive markets. Business reiterates the principle of laissez-faire and the need for the freedom to make its own decisions. The consumer movement insists on the consumer's sovereignty as a necessary element of that same doctrine. Each has been willing to admit that the other had some valid criticism, but there has been little agreement on what it is. The consumer movement can now accept, for example, the fact that advertising is a necessary part of modern merchandising. At the same time it shows its skepticism of most advertising when it characterizes as deceptive any "promotional device which deflects [the consumer's] attention away from the important competitive elements of price and quality."[17]

And, finally, its preoccupation with the sovereign consumer in the marketplace has prevented the consumer movement from relating new areas of study, particularly macroeconomic analysis and consumer marketing studies, to consumer welfare.

In macroeconomic theory, the emphasis turns from prices for individual goods in the market to the forces of total spending and total supply in the economy as a whole. In this analysis the role of the consumer shifts from allocating resources in the production of specific goods to determining the level of national income. As economic study turns from the demand schedule to the consumption function, the theory focuses on the forces determining the division of consumer income between spending and saving and seeks an explanation in such factors as the consumer's income, position in the income scale, stock of goods, expectations for the future, and family cycle.

But the consumer movement has neglected the consumer interest in terms of macroeconomic analysis. No one would dispute the consumer's interest in a level of total demand high enough to provide full employment and its assurance of a job. But where does the consumer's interest lie with regard to the different combinations of monetary and fiscal policy that can be used to achieve such a level of total demand? Were it disposed to do so, the consumer movement could advise consumers to spend or save depending on the prospect for rising or falling prices. It has been suggested, however, that even if the consumer movement did find a way to guide large numbers of consumers one way or another, it might tend to weaken the economy. Should consumers act in concert in increase or decrease the level of spending, the large shifts in spending might result in an imbalance in the economy.[18]

The consumer's interest is in both income and stable prices, but what is the consumer's interest in the conflict between policies designed to hold down inflation? In the present state of economic theory, the trade-off between employment and inflation renders the consumer's interest difficult to determine. Again, where does the consumer's interest lie in the matter of high interest rates and a tight money supply? Only in theory does restrictive monetary policy work equally against expenditures on new plant and equipment and on new private housing. What is the consumer's interest in a particular tax structure or pattern of government expenditure? These are questions raised by macroeconomic analysis that the consumer movement has not adequately considered.

In the same vein is the assertion on the part of business that selling pressure is necessary in order to generate a level of consumer demand that will provide full employment. Continually changing designs and high advertising expenditures are justified on the basis of their contribution to increased consumer spending. The consumer movement answers this from the point of view of the microeconomic consumer whose pattern of choice is distorted and for whom prices are higher. The consumer movement does not come to grips with the larger macroeconomic issue.

In much the same way, the preoccupation of microeconomic theory with the maximizing consumer inhibits the consumer movement in analyzing what the marketing studies on patterns of consumer spending and consumer motivation mean for consumers. These studies are largely the outgrowth of business's need to forge its own "informational link" with consumer. To insure a demand for the goods it produces, industry must know about people themselves, as well as about what kinds of goods people can be expected, or persuaded, to buy. This means understanding people in terms of motivation and in terms of incomes, kinds of employment, family cycle, home ownership, educational background, class identification, and leisure activity.[19]

Even though this field of study is relatively young and its proponents admit that "little is known as yet regarding why consumers act as they do," much has been done to show that consumers are not much like the knowledgeable, calculating, objective, rational consumers of economic price theory. Consumers by and large do not seem to know what they want until they see it. They are often uninterested in "useful" information about the products they buy but are open to an appeal to their unspoken desires for personal fulfillment in family or business or society. They are less concerned with getting the best value than with fulfilling myriad personal and social ambitions.

In its insistence that consumers should be rational and purposeful, the consumer movement has no way to deal with the consumer motivations that have been revealed by recent marketing studies. The movement interprets business's selling efforts as attempts to beguile consumers into buying things which otherwise they would not buy. Consumer advocates maintain that if business were to encourage objectiveness rather than irrationality, consumers would act more rationally. Even though consumer advocates may admit that consumers are sometimes emotional and irrational, they imply that consumers are encouraged to be so by business. As evidence, they point to business statements such as the following which disparage efforts to provide informative advertising: "In practice to expect rational rather than empiric decision[s] among the mass of people, in relation to the mass of low cost purchases they make each week, is ridiculous. . . ."[20]

The Lack of Alternatives

Whatever the limitations placed on the consumer movement by the acceptance of the concept of rational consumers in competitive markets, the fact of the matter is that economics offers no other working concept. This is partly because economists, generally, have neglected the area of consumption and partly because of the complex nature of consumption itself.

Although Adam Smith did say that "consumption is the sole end and purpose of all production," he went on to say that "the maxim is so self-evident that it would be absurd to attempt to prove it." Like Smith, succeeding economists assumed the importance of consumption without a great deal of analysis. In *The Scope and Method of Political Economy*, John Neville Keynes states that "a true theory of consumption [utility theory] is the keystone of political economy" and this becomes a "fundamental datum or premise of the science."[21] Joseph Dorfman notes that an early attempt by the American Economic Association to agree on "the definition of [economic] terms" broke down and "was allowed to lapse" as a result of "sharp differences . . . in the seemingly innocuous field of consumption." The differences were over the "function of consumption"—the distinction between productive and unproductive consumption and whether the study of consumption was a legitimate part of economics.[22]

Until fairly recently there was little, if any, analysis of consumption, either from the point of view of the consumer or from the point of view of the economy as a whole. The accepted theory of consumer behavior was not devised to explain consumption or the interest of the consumer but rather to explain the distribution of the returns to the factors of production. The theory of value and distribution "seeks to show how a number of circumstances taken as *given* (the fundamental data)—namely, the *preferences* and *capacities* of *individuals* and the available resources—serve to determine a structure of output and prices."[23] As the theory of demand evolved, even though consumer choices were regarded as determining the *pattern* of resource allocation, the central focus was on the *process* of allocation. Once his demand schedule was established, the consumer's role beyond his automatic response to change in price or income was not subject to analysis. The work on the theory of consumer behavior, whether through Marshall's utility analysis or the indifference and revealed preference analysis, has been to construct a theory of demand to support price analysis rather than to construct a theory that would explain consumption.

Economists have recognized the shortcomings of the accepted theory as a satisfactory explanation of consumer behavior. Such was the point of departure for Veblen, as well as for Mitchell and Kyrk. In a more recent survey article on the economics of consumption, Ruth Mack has acknowledged that a theory of demand has to be based on an understanding of how consumers decide what to buy. Yet she was unable to make any statement about the wants and choices of individual consumers other than that they are influenced by a wide variety of factors, both personal and social. And she goes on, "Whether it will be possible to fasten essential characteristics of wants and choices as now understood into a theory of consumption, the future will tell."[24]

Kenneth Boulding in *A Reconstruction of Economics* recognizes the problem too and is even less optimistic about the outcome.

The prime mover of production is consumption, and it is clear that any adequate account of the economic system must contain some consumption theory. The theory of the household and of the firm, and indeed the whole structure of economics, have been weakened by a general failure to appreciate the nature of consumption. For this reason, the present theory of the household is especially unsatisfactory. Nevertheless, it is by no means easy to formulate a worthy substitute. The theory of consumption turns out to be, rather surprising, one of the most difficult parts of economics, where it seems to be particularly hard to formulate rational principles and establish propositions from them.[25]

This "surprising" difficulty which Boulding identifies helps to suggest why nothing of any real significance was contributed to the understanding of the consumer's position by the analysis of consumption of Kyrk and others who followed her. In spite of a sizeable number of economists in the 1930s who dealt with the problem of consumption—from the point of view of standards of living, consumer choice, the maximization of consumer welfare, and the consumer-buyer in the market—twenty-five years later it could be said that there has appeared no "field of work which makes the decision making of the household the central point of inquiry."[26] And H.S. Houthakker has noted that "the theory of consumer's choice may historically have had more influence as prototype to other branches of economics than as a guide to consumption research."[27]

Dissatisfaction with such a limited analysis of consumption has, in the past fifteen years or so, led a number of economists and other social scientists to take a new tack on the study of consumption. This new approach can be said to combine general and social psychology with empirical research into consumer motivation and behavior. Such an approach seeks to go beyond the maximizing consumer with given tastes to a fuller understanding of how consumers are motivated and what determines patterns of consumer tastes and preferences. On the assumption that it is possible to measure consumer attitudes, the focus is on analyzing consumer *behavior* as the most promising means of studying consumption. This approach has been used especially in marketing studies and in the macroeconomic analysis of spending and saving. While it is generally agreed that such an approach needs to be integrated with the more traditional economic analysis, little has been done toward this end.

What Next?

In its broadest sense, I believe that the consumer movement amounts to a yearning for an improved quality of life. . ..

Senator Charles Percy
(October 1974)

What should be the specific goals for a movement whose ultimate reason for being is to increase individual consumer satisfaction? To show the limitations of the analysis of demand and consumer behavior as a rationale for the consumer movement is to leave consumer advocates without any certain prescription for the consumer's interest or role in the American economy today. From the point of view of microeconomic analysis, it is true that the consumer and his welfare can be adequately defined in terms of sovereign consumers, directing the allocation of resources through competitive markets. And, on this basis, in an economy of noncompetitive markets the consumer must be considered as impotent and disadvantaged. In this view, as Galbraith puts it, "the distribution of resources extensively reflects the power of the particular firm, . . . in company with other firms, to pursue its own purposes, . . ." rather than those of consumers.[1]

On the other hand, the fact is easily substantiated that present-day American consumers are more privileged than any in history. Indeed, a good case can be made that, given nothing more than adequate management of the national economy, consumers will continue to be well served. Higher levels of household discretionary income will increase the power of consumers to choose their own areas of spending. Moreover, as Carolyn Bell has suggested, the lack of the "purely competitive model," deplored by the consumer movement, can be said to allow the economy to respond to the "continual changes in technology and in consumer tastes and preferences." In fact, it can be argued that the American economy, through monopolistic competition and advertising, provides the variety that must be "the guidepost for economic activity," if "the 'interests of consumers' are to rule the economy."[2]

Thus consumers are at the same time both pawns in the economy and the beneficiaries of its increasing level and variety of production. But the consumer movement, with its roots in neoclassical economic theory, has been unable to accept such a paradox. It has been unable to recognize and build on the increasing material well-being that has been the good fortune of most Americans in the past three decades. Its search for consumer satisfaction has always led back to the myth of the rational consumer in competitive markets. Advocacy, legislation, education—all have been worked out within this narrow context. This suggests that if the consumer movement is to achieve its real purpose of helping consumers, it must look beyond the narrow theoretical definition of consumer to a broader understanding of what constitutes consumer satisfaction and well-being.

The Limits to Current Consumer Activity

What, then, will be the outcome of the current consumer activity? Many see it gaining momentum. They point to Nader and the activity of other consumer advocates and to the renewed interest in consumer organization and consumer education. They cite the increasing political support for consumers in both federal and state governments and the passage of legislation designed to protect and enhance the position of consumers as they act in the marketplace. Nevertheless, in spite of the increased awareness of consumers and their problems, the conclusion seems inescapable that activity and legislation directed toward the restoration of sovereign consumers will not attract widespread consumer support nor achieve any real change in the consumer's position. Given the values of most American consumers and the structure of the American economy, there is little reason to believe that any of the present efforts on behalf of consumers will achieve for them a greater sense of power or a higher level of satisfaction.

Nor is there any reason to suppose that attempts to organize consumers into an effective constituency will be any more successful in the seventies than they were in the thirties. With real incomes that have roughly doubled in the past twenty-five years, the consumer is now significantly better off than a comparison of his position with that of the "sovereign consumer" of economic theory would suggest. Even with rising prices and the recent recession, most consumers today are far more likely to be satisfied with the status quo than they were in the thirties. And, unlike the labor movement to which is is often compared, consumer organization has relatively small gains to offer the individual. There is little incentive for consumers to bear the high cost of participation in terms of time and effort when the pay-off in the form of consumer legislation or in the form of more information goes equally to participant and nonparticipant. Furthermore, given the traditional role of women as consumers and as the volunteers supporting consumer organizations, the increasing number of women workers will further narrow the base of organized consumer support. Thus there does not seem to be any great thrust for a movement of organized consumers.

The cause of consumer organization is also hurt by the lack of issues that can be the basis for sustained consumer participation and enthusiasm. Consumer issues such as the need for information and for greater protection from business duplicity have not gained widespread consumer support; at the same time, issues that do attract significant consumer support appear to have only momentary appeal and are as much a matter of historical accident as of thoughtful response to basic conditions in the economy.[3] For example, a study indicated that in 1973-1974 the primary consumer complaints were about energy and lack of integrity in government; but the main complaint the year before had been about soap![4] And even with the national economic problems at the time, a 1974-1975 study indicated that a majority of American families felt they had not suffered recent declines in their standard of living. Furthermore, the same study showed that only about 10 percent indicated "not knowing how to manage money wisely" was a problem.[5]

Mark Nadel's analysis of the political aspects of the consumer movement affirms this lack of issues.[6] Nadel maintains that consumer issues are not even generated by consumers. He holds that they are raised by activists both in and out of government who see consumer protection as a "novel and low cost" issue with a large measure of consensus. Nadel says that consumer issues are also promoted by journalists who find them useful in terms of their broad appeal. These issues provide journalists with a frame of reference in which to address not only a variety of philosophical concerns such as individuality and social responsibility in the corporate state but also more timely and easily identified problems like harmful or unsafe products and consumer deception. In Nadel's view the increased publicity given to consumer matters in recent years does not represent any new awakening on the part of consumers as a whole.

The only consumer issue that appears to have continuing viability is the tension between consumers and business. Business has tried, as far as possible, to co-opt this tension through the "marketing concept" and other efforts that are based on the principle that benefits for consumers can also be benefits for the producer.[7] When economic conditions are good, the tension between buyer and seller implicit in all market systems tends to be overlooked by consumers. But during times of economic distress, this tension becomes explicit, and consumers see the power of business as responsible for rising prices and unemployment, and they see business in general as unresponsive to the real needs and wants of consumers. By the same token, business sees consumer activity that builds on this tension as being antibusiness and, broadly interpreted, even anti-American.

It does not appear, however, that this issue of consumer versus business can be the basis for long-range consumer organization. As the Nader experience has shown, only a limited number of people are willing to take the initiative in challenging the corporate structure of American business and government. Not only is there little to be gained from any individual challenge to the present system, but there is the problem of how to effect the challenge. When the status quo is satisfactory enough, there are not many who are willing to risk it for other, unknown possibilities. Furthermore, for most consumers the continuing priority of job and income over spending means that when a choice must be made, work and production have greater appeal and support than matters of consumption.

There is also little reason to believe that consumer education will make any significant contribution to consumer organization or to political pressure on behalf of consumers. Consumer education has not been able to enlist the interest and allegiance of its students. There is a basic conflict between what most people imagine themselves to be and what consumer education says people ought to be. Its objectives are unspecified. Where it is not bound within the narrow limits of economic theory, its focus is unclear. It projects an image of consumers that is unattractive and unappealing to most Americans. Its advocates notwithstanding, consumer education as currently taught has little chance to transform people into either informed or politically active consumers.

Given the meager promise for consumer organization, consumer advocates are forced to limit their efforts largely to the political arena and to pressure for consumer legislation, and over the past decade a good deal of legislation designed to protect consumers from particular abuses has been passed. Much of this legislation deals with important matters like protection from flammable materials and unsafe food additives, and often it has been passed only after long legislative battles. But the argument can be made that by and large this legislation, at the state as well as at the federal level, has done little to change the basic position of consumers in American society. Such legislation has not significantly reduced the power and authority of the large firm over the market, and thus, although the consumer retains the ultimate choice of whether to buy, his sovereignty continues to be undermined by the mass advertising of the large firm and by the concentration of industry which weakens price competition.

It is true that consumer issues have acquired considerable political appeal. But the legislative response has been, and will probably continue to be, directed toward specific problems and of limited long-run efficacy. Recent legislation on packaging, credit costs, automobile safety, and harmful drugs are all directed toward specific practices that abuse the consumer. The costs of such legislation usually are not borne by the business involved but can be passed on to consumers. In some instances—for example, automobile safety requirements—the blame for increased prices can be put on "consumer activists" whose interference can be said to harm both consumer and producer interests. The legislation that established the National Product Safety Commission delegated to it extensive powers over consumer products found to be unsafe or harmful. But the Commission has shown relatively little ability to effect basic changes in the design and production of these goods. Furthermore, in another area of consumer concern, there is some evidence that legislated safety standards in drugs may even be detrimental to consumer well-being. This evidence suggests that the restrictions imposed by recent legislation on the development and marketing of new drugs may be costly to consumers' health.[8]

The legislation that has been passed may correct some specific consumer abuses, but it does not enhance the market power of consumers nor does it significantly curtail business initiative with regard to consumer matters. The cigarette industry is a case in point. Even in the face of widespread evidence that connects smoking with lung cancer and other health problems, the only limitation on the marketing of cigarettes has been the ban on television advertising. In the economy as a whole, as in the cigarette industry, the innovative function of what is to be produced and how it is to be marketed continues to be in the hands of business. That a new product does not "make it" is not so much a case of consumers exercising veto power in the marketplace as it is a case of business failure to sell the product effectively.

Most importantly, legislation to date has done little to break up the market power of large firms. While the control of monopoly power was the specific goal of much of Kefauver's consumer effort, legislation in this direction has made little headway. It is true that in the face of the current oil situation, there is increasing momentum in Congress to pass legislation to require the large oil companies to divest themselves of some of their oil operations. The pressure for such legislation is based on the premise that with divestiture competition in the oil industry would be increased with consequent reductions in price and increases in quantity. In a similar move, the Justice Department has filed a suit against American Telephone and Telegraph that would require it to divest itself of Western Electric. But these moves, even if successful, will not bring about significant changes if previous antitrust efforts are any indication of what will be accomplished.

What more general support for the consumer in the form of a federal consumer agency will accomplish for the consumer remains to be seen. If it is true, as some assert, that "the terms of economic transactions are set not in the marketplace . . . but in the governmental agencies through a political bargaining process . . . ,"[9] then representation of the consumer's interest before these agencies may bring about real change. General representation of this type may constitute a greater threat to business than specific remedy legislation, as its effects are less predictable and therefore less manageable. Certainly, business interests are wary of such legislation. Many see its grant of authority and its definition of the consumer interest to be so broad as to allow continual harassment of business. Even so, there is little reason to believe that individual consumers will achieve any greater sense of well-being or of satisfaction as a result of such a form of consumer representation.

But ad hoc legislation designed to remedy specific consumer problems will not restore consumer sovereignty nor basically change the consumer's position in the economy. The restoration of consumer sovereignty, as theoretically defined, would require deeper changes within the economy than would be possible, or perhaps even desirable, through any sort of legislation now contemplated.

This important point can be shown more clearly by considering the nature of some of the continuing consumer problems as they are seen by the consumer movement. In this view, the consumer is even less sovereign today than he was forty years ago. Consumer sovereignty is weakened by advertising and by the concentration of industry. It is weakened by the fact that industry no longer relies on the market as the "informational link" with the consumer but develops its own link through marketing studies and planning. Yet the tools business uses to achieve control over the market—an increasing size of enterprise and increasing use of sophisticated marketing techniques—are the same factors that in terms of the theoretical model, diminish consumer sovereignty. Restoration of consumer sovereignty would require the discontinuation of this kind of market planning.

Similarly, consumer advocates argue that consumer sovereignty is weakened by the difficulty of deciding which goods, in terms of price and quality, are a "best buy." There are almost daily additions to the numbers of complex new, and newly modeled, durable goods—cars, boats, household and electronic equipment of all kinds—whose value in terms of a quality/price comparison very few consumers are competent to make. In the category of proprietary drugs, it has been estimated that consumers have a "choice" among nearly a half-million different items. Ever larger retail units mean that the consumer is farther separated from any sort of personal contact with the seller who is responsible to his customer. New goods and large retail units, however, are the essence of a mass-consumption economy, and in a choice between them and consumer sovereignty, it is doubtful if consumers would choose the latter.

A further problem for consumer sovereignty is the persistence of social pressures operating on the consumer's buying decisions. Veblen's conspicuous consumption of the middle class is now joined by the "compensatory consumption" of low-income consumers. The pressures to buy in order to "keep up with the Joneses," to achieve status in business or sex, to display a successful life through the ability to spend money have not abated. (It can also be pointed out that these pressures have received the inadvertent blessing of macroeconomic analysis.) They are, moreover, an integral part of American culture and, like advertising, proliferation of goods, and the impersonal buyer-seller relationship, are not likely to be altered by legislation.

It should be clear that the restoration of consumer sovereignty, in the context of economic theory, is not possible in the modern American economy. To restore the consumer to his "rightful" role in the economy would require markets where rational consumers bargain with competing producers. Neither of these conditions is any longer possible in a mass-consumption economy that depends on consumers who can be persuaded to buy the wide variety of goods and services developed and made available by large firms.

A Revisionist View

What is most needed, from the consumer point of view, is a clearer understanding of what is the consumer's best interest in the modern industrial economy. A new set of questions should be addressed. What should be consumer goals in an economy which so far has provided for most of its consumers an increasingly large quantity of goods and services and which now faces the prospect of a stable, if not declining, level of production? How are consumers to relate to the increased pressures for a more equal distribution of income? How are future goals to be shaped by society's heightened sense of corporate responsibility for both the physical and social environment? What are effective means to a sense of community and to personal identity and responsibility in an economy characterized by increasingly specialized roles organized in ever more complex private and public bureaucracies?

These are the questions that matter, but the consumer movement has not been able to turn to them because it has been limited by the sterile and unreal concept of the economic consumer. This concept has kept the consumer movement tied to a quantitative view of consumption, based on given consumer wants, which has cut it off from the larger issue of consumer well-being and the means to increase it.

To call for the consumer movement to free itself from the narrow view of economic theory is much easier than to define what its broader view should be. After all, aside from the radical Marxist analysis, the neoclassical view is the only one around. At the same time criticism of this sort carries with it the obligation to look for and propose alternatives, even if they fall short of providing a new and acceptable rationale. In undertaking this obligation, one can point to several areas of concern in which consumer advocates might find the beginnings of a deeper understanding of consumer problems and issues that would hold the promise of bringing forth significant consumer response. Consumer education along these lines would help people begin to understand that the role of consumption in their own lives and in society is far more important and complex than the simple mechanics of buying might suggest.

The increasing interdependence of modern society means that consumers can no longer be viewed as isolated individuals capable of independently achieving their own material well-being. Interdependency is the direct result of the increasing level of specialization and of the division of labor in the large scale of production made possible by modern technology. These same factors have, of course, also been the source of much of the world's economic growth during the past 200 years. In emphasizing the problems and dissatisfaction with the *things* consumers buy, the consumer movement has ignored the fact that, for most people in the United States today, the consumer problem is not maximizing individual satisfaction in terms of goods and services, but it is the economic complexity which has itself made possible the increasing quantities of goods and services. The consumer problem today is how to cope with this complexity.

In a highly specialized economy there is a direct connection between the level of interdependency and the fact that there is more and more in peoples' lives that is "material," i.e., that is measured in money. As industrialization proceeds, more and more formerly "personal" or "home" production becomes specialized and subject to the market. Interdependency increases and self-sufficiency decreases as care for the young and the aged become specialized and monetized, and as housewives' services come to be computed in monetary terms. It is a paradox that as more and more of life's components become market-oriented and thus subject to calculation in terms of consumer goods and services purchased, there is a greater interdependency that restricts the ability of the individual to provide independently for his total well-being. This is no small frustration for people in a society whose value system is rooted in individualism.

Increasing specialization has brought other frustrations as well. One of these is money. Money as a substitute for barter is a rational accompaniment to the higher levels of production and output resulting from specialization. And it is only logical that as the standard of living goes up, more and more in people's lives has to be reckoned in terms of money. But Americans have a double standard about money: They are willing to say that money counts; at the same time they are reluctant to say that it is the only thing that counts. Thus the increasing pervasiveness of money which is the result of increased specialization and production is a source of conflict about its importance as "a measure of all things" in people's lives. In the minds of most people, money is not just a means to more goods and services; money has also become a phenomenon of complex psychological significance. Personal money matters have become a subject about which people do not wish to speak openly; they have supplanted sex as the socially forbidden subject. But the consumer movement, in its emphasis on what goods and services money will buy, has ignored the very real but uncertain feelings people have about money.

Similarly, much of the frustration in the lives of people as consumers, which comes from dealing with large private or public bureaucracies, is also related to the level of specialization and scale of production. The myriad tasks into which production is divided necessarily require coordination. In simplest terms this coordination is bureaucracy. Similarly, the scale of production that dwarfs the individual and his choices is also directly related to increases in total output. Consumers are at cross-purposes when, on the one hand, they bemoan the impersonality and size of organization and, on the other, call for an ever increasing level and variety of goods and services. The salesperson who cannot explain why a complicated consumer product is not working properly, as well as the complicated product itself, are both the results of specialization and mass production.

That consumer problems are increasingly social rather than material is borne out by a recent study which indicates that people are not so worried about what happens to them as individuals as they are about how to cope with collective problems.[10] The concern of an increasing number of American families seems to be less with problems of how to promote their own material well-being than with problems associated with interdependency and large-scale organization over which they as individuals have little control. According to the study, people are worried about inflation, depression, and lack of self-sufficiency. All these are collective problems of interdependency and cannot be solved by independent and efficient consumers. If the consumer movement will look beyond the neo-classical economic model, it can move away from the very limiting assumption that wants are individually and independently determined. If consumer wants are socially determined then, as one writer put it, wants "no longer are sacred, . . . [which] means that the restriction or reshaping of wants is not a mortal sin."[11] This would allow a consumer movement freedom to suggest which kinds of consumption are "better" or "worse" than others. It would give a consumer movement the authority it now lacks to criticize advertising. It would provide the consumer movement with the opportunity to deal with social consumption.

To recognize that wants are socially determined, that is, that they are formed out of all the bits of information that come to people from whatever sources and out of whatever needs and desires, would, as much as anything else, free a consumer movement from the dominance of business. As long as wants are seen as independently determined or given, then any attempt to change wants or to intervene on the consumer's side of the market can be said to be an illegitimate invasion of personal choice. Business has never seen its manipulation of consumer wants through advertising and other marketing in this light; indeed, it can be said that business sees its relationship with consumers as a privileged one, rather like that between the physician and the patient. So, as Galbraith has put it, "public objections to lethal automobile design, disabling drugs, disfiguring beauty aids . . . are interference with the individual's design for maximizing his satisfaction." And all of this is "in the name of the individual."[12] Once it is accepted that wants are not independently determined, then a consumer movement could criticize advertising for what it really is—an attempt to manipulate people to behave in a certain way. Furthermore, a consumer movement would then be in a position to make the case for certain kinds of consumption over others, whether because of what certain products did to consumers or to the environment or to the workers who produced them. That the consumer movement could become an advocate for certain kinds of consumption would not deny the similar—and long-exercised—right of advocacy to business. It is just that there could then be advocacy on more than one side.

Such advocacy would be particularly useful in the case of social consumption that, in the final analysis, is a political issue. When the consumer movement is no longer bound to the notion of the maximization of individual combinations of goods and services as the consumer's goal, it can deal with means by which more social comsumption may yield a higher level of satisfaction than more individual consumption. It can deal with the issue of private goods versus social goods, as well as with issues about choosing among different kinds of social goods.

It is ironic that Alfred Marshall, whose work more than any other has shaped microeconomic theory, saw the limitation which individually determined, and therefore given, choices imposed on the analysis of consumption. In particular, he was concerned with the question of whether maximum satisfaction would actually be achieved by leaving to each person the choice to spend his income in whatever way he liked. Through the concept of consumer surplus, he showed how increases in consumer welfare could be possible by rearranging the production and consumption of certain goods. Marshall never recommended any specific government action to achieve these ends, but he did not flinch from suggesting such a possibility.

Finally, any consumer movement must come to grips with the question of relative shares of income. So far, the consumer movement in the United States has ignored the issue of consumer satisfaction when there are inequalities in purchasing power. Partly, this is because of its reliance on an economic model that has very little to say about relative incomes, but, just as importantly, it is because Americans in general have not faced up to the conflict between people's worth in terms of their humanity and in terms of their incomes. Americans have not been willing to deal with the issue of income and equality.

Yet the intuitive feeling of most people that what really matters, in terms of who people are, is what material possessions they have in relation to others is reinforced by a good deal of scholarly evidence. Seventy-five years ago Veblen pointed out that much of the reward for consumption came from the ability to demonstrate by "conspicuous consumption" that one person had a higher income than another. Macroeconomics has recognized the importance of relative incomes by building into the theory of consumer demand the assumption that consumers in their spending try to hold onto what they see as their place in a hierarchy of levels of consumption.[13] In a more recent study, Richard A. Easterlin maintains that more money buys more "happiness" primarily when it puts one person ahead of another.[14]

This evidence that it is less what people have in the way of absolute quantities of goods than what they have relative to others which makes them feel more or less satisfied undermines a basic premise of a consumer movement, namely, that greater quantities of goods and services increase satisfaction and well-being. If goods can be equated with satisfaction only when they put one person ahead of someone else, then to suggest that wise consumption for all can make everybody better off is rather like suggesting that if everyone in a stadium stands up, everyone can see better. One person gets "ahead" only when others do not.[15]

This unwillingness to face up to the issue of relative incomes has been one of the stumbling blocks in the way of providing consumer education to people with low incomes. All that consumer educators have been able to say is that if people spend "wisely" what income they have, then they can have more nutritious meals, get taken advantage of less by unscrupulous merchants, or be less in debt. But such consumer "wisdom" denies to low-income families the areas of spending by which they seek to compensate for their low social status. For example, given a choice, it is probably a safe bet that most people in debt would rather be in debt with the goods they get in debt to pay for than free of debt and without the car or TV or set of living room furniture. People do not lose much status by being in debt; but without goods they do not have any status at all. The problems that come to mind when one suggests that consumer education should help people understand how it really is in a society that equates goods with status indicates the ambivalence with which Americans deal with the question of people's human worth and their economic worth.

More importantly, this issue of shares of income is going to become more difficult as time goes on. It is rather commonly agreed today that the important economic question is not so much that of the production of goods as it is of their distribution. As long as there can be a high level of economic growth, it is possible for everyone to have an absolutely larger consumption of goods and services. In such circumstances, there is likely to be less concern over relative shares. But with a slowing down of growth, which many predict will continue, this will no longer be the case. With a slowing of growth and of the increase in absolute quantities, there will be increasing tension over shares. The real question for any consumer-oriented program is how the total "pie" can be divided up and still make people satisfied with what they have. It is worth noting that in any society geared to the individual, more for some people necessarily means less for others.

The common thread of this revisionist view is the problem of an individualistically oriented consumer in a world that is increasingly interdependent. Neoclassical economic analysis focuses on unrelated consumers each seeking to maximize individual total satisfaction through buying various combinations of goods in the market. But an analysis of interdependence is equally important in any efforts to help consumers understand themselves and the role of consumption in their lives.

The problem of the individual versus the polity, or of freedom versus social control has, of course, deep philosophical roots. Among economists the concern for social well-being has found its most recent expression in the discussion about how best to deal with the externalities associated with economic growth. Here the question is how to resolve the conflict between the benefits of growth that can be individually distributed and the costs of economic growth that are difficult to attribute and that have wide social impact. This is but one aspect of the larger question of how to move from a world where there is a limitless frontier to one in which the boundaries are known and all must live within them. (Kenneth Boulding pictures this problem most vividly in his figure of the earth as a self-contained spaceship.) The question of the social structure of this new kind of world has been most carefully explored by Daniel Bell in his *The Coming of the Post-Industrial Society*. Bell writes:

[T]he consumer-oriented free-enterprise society no longer satisfies the citizenry. .. This is a society that has rested on the premises of individualism and market rationality, in which the varied ends desired by individuals would be maximized by free exchange. We now move to a communal ethic, without that community being . . . wholly defined.[16]

By and large, however, the social sciences, and especially economics, have continued to work within the framework of "individualism and market rationality," and have posed the conflicts between individualism and social interdependency as "problems" to be solved. Accordingly, we have the "problem" of the very large corporation, which has now become the "problem" of the multinational corporation, the "problem" of urban sprawl or the "problem" of poverty. These are not "problems" in the sense of arithmetic problems in which we know what to do to solve them. All of these "problems" are the result of the social impact of individual decisions. They are "problems" in the sense that they are difficult and complex, and, in the end, they are "problems" because they are unsolvable by presently accepted modes of thought which explain society in terms of the individual.

Thus, the consumer movement has enunciated the "problem" of large-scale enterprise. For the individual consumer, the problem is one of prices and quantities of goods and services, and the need, somehow, to achieve the prices and quantities that approximate those under perfect competition. But given the present scale of production, it is unimaginable that these conditions could ever be achieved. The real problem of the very large corporation is not a question of prices or of producer versus consumer but the question of the power of the large enterprise in the context of the total society, not only of the nation but increasingly of the world.

To suggest that a "revisionist" consumer movement can find the solutions to these perplexing problems on its own would be absurd. But it might be possible for a consumer movement, instead of representing the self-centered, sober, penny-pinching consumer, to join with others in analyzing the relation of consumption to the quality of life. In raising these kinds of issues, consumer education stands a good chance of being more widely accepted and the consumer movement stands a chance of gaining a constituency.

Notes

Notes

Chapter 1

1. Persia Campbell, *The Consumer Interest: A Study in Consumer Economics* (New York: Harper & Bros., 1949), p. 618. Dr. Campbell points out that though consumer groups may differ on specific issues, "all consumer organizations aim at raising . . . the level of consumption." (Ibid.)

2. Houthakker states, "The subject matter of economics . . . is the mutual adjustment of means and ends," and he goes on to point out that for the purpose of economic analysis, it is enough to say that consumption is determined by prices and income. (H.S. Houthakker, "An Economist's Approach to the Study of Spending," in *Household Decision-Making,* ed. Nelson H. Foote, Vol. IV of *Consumer Behavior* (New York: New York University Press, 1961), pp. 127-128. This does not rule out, however, the need for the larger study of consumption from the point of view of the consumer.

Chapter 2

1. Adam Smith, *The Wealth of Nations,* Vol. 2 (New York: Everyman's Library, E.P. Dutton, 1910), p. 155.

2. Jerome Rothenberg states that W. H. Hutt "coined the title, if not the substance of the concept of 'consumer sovereignty.' " ["Consumers' Sovereignty Revisited and the Hospitality of Freedom of Choice," *American Economic Review, Papers and Proceedings,* Vol. 52 (May 1962), p. 269]. In *Economists and the Public* (London: Jonathan Cape, 1936), Hutt compared the power of the sovereignty of the consumer to the sovereignty of the voter through the ballot box. He says that the "consumer is sovereign when, in his role of citizen, he has not delegated to political institutions for authoritarian use the power which he can exercise socially through the power to demand (or to refrain from demanding)." Hutt goes on to say that "we believe that the achievements of the productive system can be measured only in terms of the extent to which they represent a response to consumers' will" (pp. 257-258). Though this was exactly the position of the consumer movement, there is no mention of Hutt in the consumer literature.

3. Alfred Marshall, *Principles of Economics,* 8th ed. (London: Macmillan, 1930), p. 95.

4. Ibid., pp. 26-27.

5. Ibid., p. 85.

6. Ibid., p. 91, n. 1.

7. Ibid., p. 83.

8. Ibid., p. 89.

9. Ibid., p. 137.

10. Thorstein Veblen, *The Theory of the Leisure Class* (New York: Macmillan, 1915), p. 25.

11. Ibid., p. 126.

12. Ibid., p. 157.

13. First published in *American Economic Review,* Vol. 2 (June 1912). Reprinted in Wesley C. Mitchell, *The Backward Art of Spending Money* (New York: Augustus M. Kelley, 1950).

14. Ibid., p. 3.

15. Ibid., p. 4.

16. That traditional theory always posits a rational man is but another difficulty in using it to analyze modern consumption. To substitute *housewife* for *consumer* in the propositions of demand theory is to suggest some of the implications. For an interesting discussion of this point, see John Kenneth Galbraith, *Economics and the Public Purpose* (Boston: Houghton Mifflin, 1973). Chapters IV and XXIII.

17. Mitchell, *Backward Art,* p. 10.

18. Ibid., p. 16.

19. Ibid., p. 9.

20. Hazel Kyrk, *A Theory of Consumption* (Boston: Houghton Mifflin, 1923).

21. Hazel Kyrk, "The Development of the Field of Consumption," *Journal of Marketing,* Vol. 4 (July 1939), p. 16.

22. In the past twenty years, however, interdisciplinary study of consumption has been growing. See, for example, the various volumes in the *Consumer Behavior Series,* eds. Lincoln H. Clark and Nelson Foote, sponsored by the Committee for Research on Consumer Attitudes and Behavior, (New York: New York University Press, 1954), or *Family Economic Behavior: Problems and Prospects,* ed. Eleanor B. Sheldon, (Philadelphia: J.B. Lippincott, 1973).

23. Adolf A. Berle, Jr., and Gardiner C. Means, *The Modern Corporation and Private Property* (New York: Macmillan, 1932).

24. Edward H. Chamberlin, *The Theory of Monopolistic Competition* (Cambridge, Massachusetts:Harvard University Press, 1933). And simultaneously in England from the publication *The Economics of Imperfect Competition* by Joan Robinson (London: Macmillan, 1933).

25. Berle and Means, *The Modern Corporation,* p. 351.

26. Gardiner C. Means, "The Consumer and the New Deal," *The Annals of the American Academy of Political and Social Science,* Vol. 173 (May 1934), p. 12. (Cited hereafter as *The Annals,* Vol. 173.) In a study completed forty years later, Means comes to the same conclusions. See "The New Monopolies," *Consumer Reports* (April 1975), p. 379.

27. Ruby T. Norris, *The Theory of Consumer's Demand* (New Haven, Connecticut: Yale University Press, 1941), p. 151.

Chapter 3

1. F.J. Schlink, *Your Money's Worth* (New York: Macmillan, 1927). The book was subtitled "A Study of the Waste of the Consumer's Dollar."

2. Ibid., p. 2.

3. Robert S. Lynd, "Family Members as Consumers," *The Annals of the American Academy of Political and Social Science,* Vol. 160 (March 1932), p. 87.

4. Stuart Chase, *The Tragedy of Waste* (New York: Grosset and Dunlap, 1925), p. 113.

5. Sumner Slichter, *Modern Economic Society* (New York: Henry Holt and Co., 1928), p. 564.

6. Robert S. Lynd, "The Consumer Becomes a 'Problem,' " *The Annals,* Vol. 173, p. 5. This volume, titled "The Ultimate Consumer" and edited by J.G. Brainerd, was an excellent statement of the scope and variety of consumer problems. It included a variety of articles on the consumer's position in the economy, the need for standards in consumers' goods, problems of advertising and marketing as they affect the consumer, and the need for government to assume some responsibility in the consumer's behalf.

7. Persia Campbell, *Consumer Representation in the New Deal* (New York: Columbia University Press, 1940), pp. 107-109.

8. *The New York Times* (December 17, 1933).

9. Edwin G. Nourse, Joseph S. Davis, and John D. Black, *Three Years of the Agricultural Adjustment Administration* (Washington, D.C.: The Brookings Institution, 1937), p. 39.

10. Ibid., p. 393.

11. Ibid., p. 395.

12. U.S. National Bituminous Coal Commission, The Consumers' Counsel, *Protection for Consumers of Bituminous Coal,* 1938.

13. Ibid.

14. See Ellis W. Hawley, *The New Deal and the Problem of Monopoly* (Princeton, New Jersey: Princeton University Press, 1966), pp. 198-200, and Arthur M. Schlesinger, Jr., *The Age of Roosevelt, I: The Crisis of the Old Order, 1919-1933* (Boston: Houghton Mifflin, 1957), pp. 52, 74, and 76.

15. Cited as Appendix II in Campbell, *Consumer Representation in the New Deal,* p. 290.

16. Arthur Kallet and F.J. Schlink, *100,000,000 Guinea Pigs* (New York: Vanguard Press, 1932); M.C. Phillips, *Skin Deep* (New York: Vanguard Press, 1934); and F.J. Schlink, *Eat, Drink, and Be Wary* (Washington, D.C.: Consumers' Research Inc., 1935).

17. C.E. Warne, "Consumer Education — A National Responsibility," in National Conference on Consumer Education, *Consumer Education for Life Problems* (Columbia, Missouri: Institute for Consumer Education, 1941), p. 199.

18. "Comment," *Journal of Home Economics,* vol. 36 (April 1944), p. 222.

19. Jessie V. Coles, *Standards and Labels for Consumers' Goods* (New York: The Ronald Press, 1949), p. 352. See also U.S. House of Representatives, *Hearings Before the Special Committee to Investigate Executive Agencies,* 78th Cong., 1st sess. (1943).

20. See Thomas C. Cochran, *The American Business System* (Cambridge, Massachusetts: Harvard University Press, 1965), p. 157ff., and Francis X. Sutton et al., *The American Business Creed* (Cambridge, Massachusetts: Harvard University Press, 1956), pp. 139-140.

21. Cf. Mary Jean Bowman, "The Consumer in the History of Economic Doctrine," *American Economic Review, Papers and Proceedings,* Vol. 41 (May 1951), p. 16.

22. *New York Times* (January 18, 1947).

23. The hearings ran for nearly seven years. There were in all some twenty-nine volumes of hearings. From the point of view of Kefauver's espousal of the consumer's cause, the most useful volumes are the following: U.S. Senate Subcommittee on Antitrust and Monopoly of the Committee on Judiciary, *Hearings, Administered Prices,* 85th Cong., 1st sess. (1957); Part 1. *Opening Phase – Economists Views;* Parts 9 and 10, *Alternative Public Policies,* 86th Cong., 1st sess. (1959); *A Compendium on Public Policy,* 88th Cong., 1st sess. (1963). A readable account of Kefauver's views of the hearings, begun by Kefauver and completed after his death by Irene Till, is *In A Few Hands* (New York: Pantheon Books, 1965).

24. *New York Times* (November 11, 1959).

25. Julius F. Rothman, "How the AFL-CIO Helps to Inform Consumers," Council on Consumer Information, *Selected Proceedings, Sixth Annual Conference* (1960). See also, "A Lesson from Cranberries," *Consumer Reports* (January 1960), p. 47.

26. *New Republic* (January 19, 1963), p. 2.

Chapter 4

1. Thomas F. Hogarty, "Survey of Non-Federal Consumer Groups," *Consumer Affairs* (Summer 1975), p. 112.

2. John Cassels in *Consumer Education: Why and How,* Proceedings of a Conference on Consumer Education, George Peabody College for Teachers, May 1940 (Nashville, Tennessee: George Peabody College for Teachers, 1940), p. 20.

3. A term used by Mark V. Nadel in *The Politics of Consumer Protection* (New York: Bobbs-Merrill, 1971), p. 41.

4. U.S. Congress, Senate, Subcommittee of the Committee on Banking and Currency, *Hearings, Truth in Lending 1963-64,* 88th Cong., 1st sess. (1964), p. 1487.

5. U.S. Congress, Senate, Subcommittee on Antitrust and Monopoly of the Committee of the Judiciary, *Hearings, Packaging and Labeling Practices,* 87th Cong., 1st sess. 1961, p. 2. The first Congressional hearing on the matter in 1961 was to investigate the need for control over packaging and labeling. There were hearings on specific legislative proposals in 1963, and again in 1965.

6. Ibid., p. 193. The fact of the matter is, however, that they cannot. A 1974 study by the Education Commission of the States shows that a majority of American adults have only limited ability to do "consumer math."

7. Ibid., p. 495.

8. *Consumer Reports* (February 1967), p. 114.

9. See T. David McCullough, "A Unit Pricing Test" in *The Economics of Consumer Protection* ed. Loys L. Mather (Danville, Ohio: The Interstate, 1971), pp. 131-137.

10. *National Journal Reports* (May 3, 1975), p. 659.

11. *Newsweek* (January 28, 1974), p. 66.

12. *National Journal Reports* (May 3, 1975), p. 659.

13. Peter H. Schuck of Consumers Union in testimony at the Senate Hearing, March 28, 1973. Quoted in *Congressional Digest* (November 1974), p. 282.

14. Ibid.

15. Cf. Edie Fraser, "Consumer Legislative Update," *Business and Society Review* (Winter 1974-75), pp. 58-63.

16. "An Official Consumer Voice in Washington," *Consumer Reports* (September 1962), p. 463.

17. U.S. Office of the President, Consumer Advisory Council, *First Report* (October 1963), p. 9.

18. *The New Republic* (November 2, 1963), p. 5.

19. *Advertising Age* (March 13, 1967), p. 40.

20. Lyndon B. Johnson, "Special Message to the Congress on Consumer Interests," February 5, 1964, *Public Papers of the Presidents,* 1963-64, Book I (Washington, D.C.: Government Printing Office, 1965), p. 264.

21. U.S., Office of the President, Consumer Advisory Council, *Consumer Issues '66* (June 12, 1966).

22. Ibid., p. 34.

23. Charles L. Gould, "Advertising" (address before a Conference of the Advertising Federation of America, February 8, 1967), *Vital Speeches,* May 1, 1967, p. 437. Reprinted with permission.

24. *Printers Ink* (September 11, 1964), p. 71.

25. "Special Report," Memo from Esther Peterson to the President, The Regional Consumer Conferences: Comments, Conclusions, Recommendations (n.d.).

26. "The Unmaking of a Consumer Advocate," *Consumer Reports* (February 1972), p. 80.

27. American Council on Consumer Interests, *Newsletter* (September 1975).

28. ACCI, *Newsletter* (January 1974).

29. State of Colorado, Colorado Legislative Council, *Consumer Problems in Colorado,* Research Publication 112, 1966, p. 143.

30. Hogarty, "Non-Federal Consumer Groups," p. 109.

31. Arch W. Troelstrup, *The Consumer in American Society* (New York: McGraw-Hill, 1974), p. 616. This book has an excellent summary of governmental support for the consumer at the state and local level. A yearly summary *State Consumer Action* is published by the Office of Consumer Affairs, Department of Health, Education, and Welfare (Washington, D.C.: Government Printing Office).

32. State of Colorado, Metropolitan Denver District Attorneys' Consumer Office, *Year-End Report, March 1, 1974–February 28, 1975,* mimeographed.

33. Colorado Legislative Council, *Consumer Problems,* p. 134.

34. Ibid.

35. U.S. Congress, Senate, Subcommittee on Reorganization, Research and International Organization of the Committee on Government Operation and the Subcommittee on Consumers of the Committee on Commerce, *Joint Hearings, To Establish an Independent Consumer Protection Agency,* 93rd Cong., 1st sess., 1973, p. 165.

36. *Wall Street Journal* (January 11, 1972).

Chapter 5

1. Ralph Nader, *Unsafe at Any Speed* (New York: Grossman Publishers, 1965), p. xi.

2. Ibid., p. 345.

3. Mark V. Nadel, *The Politics of Consumer Protection* (New York: Bobbs-Merrill, 1971), pp. 41, 142.

4. Ralph Nader, "Nader on Nuclear Alternatives," *New York Times Magazine* (March 24, 1974), p. 8.

5. *Business Week* (January 11, 1969), p. 36.

6. Richard Armstrong, "The Passion That Rules Ralph Nader," *Fortune* (May 1971), p. 226.

7. Ralph Nader, ed., *The Consumer and Corporate Accountability* (New York: Harcourt Brace Jovanovich, 1973), pp. 215–216.

8. For a careful summary of the various branches of the Nader establishment, see Susan Gross, "The Nader Network," *Business and Society Review* (Spring 1975), pp. 5–15.

9. Ibid., p. 6.

10. Armstrong, "The Passion That Rules Ralph Nader," p. 220.

11. Ralph Nader, "A Citizen's Guide to the American Economy," *New York Review* (September 2, 1971), p. 14. Reprinted with permission from *New York Review of Books,* copyright © 1971, Nyrev Inc.

12. Ibid.

13. Ibid., p. 16.

14. Nader, *The Consumer and Corporate Accountability,* p. 89.

15. Ralph Nader and Aileen Coward, "Claims Without Substance" in Nader, *The Consumer and Corporate Accountability,* pp. 90–97.

16. Ralph Nader, "The Free Market and Other Myths," *Business and Society Review* (Summer 1972), pp. 29–33.

17. Nader, "A Citizen's Guide," p. 17. Reprinted with permission from *New York Review of Books,* copyright © 1971, Nyrev Inc.

18. Ibid.

19. Ralph Nader, "The Burned Children" in Nader, *The Consumer and Corporate Accountability,* p. 59.

20. Nader, "The Free Market and Other Myths," p. 31.

21. Ralph Nader, "The Case for Federal Chartering," *Corporate Power in America* (New York: Grossman Publishers, 1973). The discussion of Nader's proposal for federal chartering draws on this paper.

22. Ibid., p. 68.

23. Nader, "The Free Market and Other Myths," pp. 32–33.

24. Nader, *The Consumer and Corporate Accountability,* p. 311.

25. Ibid.

26. Ibid., p. viii.

27. Thomas Whiteside, *The New Yorker* (October 8, pp. 50–111, and October 15, 1973, pp. 46–101).

28. Nader, "The Free Market and Other Myths," p. 32.

29. Ralph Nader, "Action for a Change," in *The Consumer and Corporate Accountability,* p. 370.

30. Ibid.

31. Ibid., p. 371.

32. Ibid., p. 369.

33. Ibid., p. 370.

34. Nader, "A Citizen's Guide," p. 15.

35. Armstrong, "The Passion That Rules Ralph Nader," p. 145.

36. Nader, "A Citizen's Guide . . . ," p. 14.

37. *New York Times* (August 23, 1975).

38. Nader, *The Consumer and Corporate Accountability,* p. xii.

39. Alan Reynolds, "What Does Ralph Nader Really Want?" *National Review* (February 28, 1975), pp. 219–223.

40. See Peter H. Aranson, "Federal Chartering of Corporations: An Idea Worth Forgetting," *Business and Society Review* (Winter 1973), pp. 59–64.

41. Reynolds, "What Does Ralph Nader Really Want?" p. 220.

42. Aranson, "Federal Chartering of Corporations," p. 64.

43. *Newsweek* (February 19, 1973), p. 70.

44. Reynolds, "What Does Ralph Nader Really Want?" p. 222.

45. Ibid.

118

46. *The Wall Stret Journal* (May 22, 1975), p. 14.

47. *National Journal Reports* (July 12, 1975), p. 1028.

48. Senator John G. Tower, as quoted in *U.S. News and World Report* (April 28, 1975), p. 59.

49. H. Bruce Palmer, "Progressive Enterprise" in *Business and the Consumer* (Washington, D.C.: The American University, 1971), p. 49.

50. Ibid.

51. John Kenneth Galbraith's *The New Industrial State* (Boston: Houghton Mifflin, 1967) is probably the most effective statement of this position.

52. Nader, "A Citizen's Guide," pp. 17–18.

53. Ralph Nader, "The Man in the Class Action Suit," *Rolling Stone* (November 20, 1975), p. 54.

54. For another version of this argument, see E.F. Schumacher, *Small is Beautiful: Economics as if People Mattered* (New York: Harper & Row, 1973).

55. *Rolling Stone,* p. 54.

56. Ibid., p. 55.

57. Ibid.

58. Nader, "Action for a Change," p. 369.

Chapter 6

1. *Wall Street Journal* (April 9, 1975), p. 1.

2. Cf. Consumer Federation of America, *Directory of State and Local Consumer Groups,* (Washington, D.C., January, 1975).

3. *Consumer Reports* (November 1966), p. 572.

4. *Consumers' Research Magazine* (August 1974), p. 3.

5. *Consumer Reports* (February 1975), p. 72.

6. *Wall Street Journal* (May 9, 1975), p. 1.

7. *Consumer Reports* (September 1975), p. 525.

8. *Consumer Reports* (February 1975), p. 72.

9. *Consumer Reports* (September 1975), p. 524.

10. *American Federationist* (November 1973), p. 27.

11. Sidney Margolis in *The American Federationist* (March 1974), p. 21.

12. *Wall Street Journal* (April 9, 1975), p. 1.

13. Solomon Barkin, "Trade Unions and Consumerism," *Journal of Economic Issues* (June 1973), pp. 317–321.

14. Ibid., p. 321.

15. Clinton L. Warne, "The Consumer Movement and the Labor Movement," *Journal of Economic Issues* (June 1973), pp. 307–316.

16. The proceedings of these annual conferences were published by the Institute for Consumer Education, Columbia, Missouri, as *Next Steps in Consumer Education* (1939), *Making Consumer Education Effective* (1940), and *Consumer Education for Life Problems* (1941).

17. Herbert A. Tonne, *Consumer Education in the Schools* (New York: Prentice-Hall, 1941), p. xiii.

18. National Association of Secondary School Principals, *Consumer Education in Your School: A Handbook for Teachers and Administrators* (Washington, D.C.: National Association of Secondary School Principals, 1947), p. 19.

19. Elisha Gray II, "Educating the Consumer," in The Conference Board, *The Challenge of Consumerism* (New York: The Conference Board, Inc., 1971), p. 79.

20. Consumers Union of U.S., Inc., Consumer Education Materials Project (Mt. Vernon, New York: 1973).

21. V.T. Thayer, *Formative Ideas in American Education* (New York: Dodd, Mead, 1965), p. 281.

22. *Consumer Reports* (March 1971), p. 133.

23. David Caplovitz, *The Poor Pay More* (New York: The Free Press of Glencoe, 1963), p. 13.

24. D.I. Padberg, "Today's Consumer," in *The Economics of Consumer Protection* ed. Loys L. Mather (Danville, Ohio: The Interstate, 1971), pp. 11-21.

25. Gerhard Scherf, "Consumer Education as a Means of Alleviating Dissatisfaction," *Journal of Consumer Affairs* (Summer 1974), pp. 61-75.

Chapter 7

1. See, for example, Mary Gardiner Jones, "Planning the Federal Trade Commissioner's Consumer Protection Activities," *Journal of Consumer Affairs* (Summer 1974), pp. 8-29; Mark V. Nadel, *The Politics of Consumer Protection* (New York: Bobbs-Merrill, 1971); Rex H. Warland in his review of Barbara B. Murray, *Consumerism* in *Journal of Consumer Affairs* (Summer 1974), pp. 111-112.

2. Office of Consumer Affairs, *An Approach to Consumer Education for Adults* (Washington, D.C.: Government Printing Office, January 1, 1973), p. 3.

3. See, for example, Steffan B. Linder's, *The Harried Leisure Class* (New York: Columbia University Press, 1970), for an analysis of the demands on time in modern high-consumption societies.

4. Stacy May, "The Work Most Needed in the Next Five Years," *Next Steps in Consumer Education,* National Conference on Consumer Education (Columbia, Missouri: Institute for Consumer Education, 1939), p. 175.

5. Quotes in *Consumer Reports* (May 1972), p. 270.

6. "Is War on Poverty Becoming War on Business?" *Nation's Business* (March 1966), p. 59.

7. See, for instance, Tibor Scitovsky, "On the Principle of Consumers' Sovereignty," *Papers on Welfare and Growth* (Stanford, California: Stanford University Press, 1964), or Mary Jane Bowman, "The Consumer in the History of Economic Doctrine," *American Economic Review, Papers and Proceedings* (May 1951), pp. 1-18.

8. Richard W. Darrow, "Super Protection, Who Wants It?" (Address, Television Bureau of Advertising, New York, November 15, 1967.) *Vital Speeches,* January 1, 1968, p. 172. Reprinted with permission.

9. Maurice H. Stans in *The Challenge of Consumerism,* p. 2.

10. Advertisement sponsored by the Magazine Publishers Association, appearing in *Newsweek* (February 27, 1967), p. 95.

11. Senator John G. Tower in *U.S. News and World Report* (April 4, 1975) p. 60.

12. Jack McCroskey, "An Optimist Looks at the Economy," *University of Denver Magazine,* Vol. 4 (March 1967), p. 18.

13. This helpful phrase appears in Harry R. Tosdale, "Bases for the Study of Consumer Demand," *Journal of Marketing,* Vol. 4 (July 1939).

14. Ibid., p. 3.

15. Ibid., pp. 4, 8. Speaking in 1939, Tosdale criticized the consumer movement for not helping consumers tell producers what they did want.

16. Edward L. Bond, Jr., in The Conference Board, *The Challenge of Consumerism,* p. 42.

17. Mary Gardiner Jones in *The Challenge of Consumerism,* p. 88.

18. Statement of George Katona at 1961 hearings, reprinted in *Hearings on Truth in Lending, 1963-64,* p. 1491.

19. See, for example, Thomas S. Robertson, *Consumer Behavior* (Glenview, Illinois: Scott, Foresman 1970).

20. Quoted in *Consumer Reports* (March 1972), p. 134.

21. John Neville Keynes, *The Scope and Method of Political Economy,* 4th ed. (New York: Augustus M. Kelley, Bookseller, 1963), p. 111.

22. Joseph Dorfman, *The Economic Mind in American Civilization,* Vol. 3 (New York: Viking Press, 1959), pp. 208-209.

23. R.F. Harrod, "The Scope and Method of Economics," *Economic Journal,* Vol. 49 (September 1938):386. Emphasis added.

24. Ruth P. Mack, "Economics of Consumption" in *A Survey of Contemporary Economics,* ed. Bernard F. Haley (Homewood, Illinois: Richard D. Irwin, 1952), p. 48.

25. Kenneth Boulding, *A Reconstruction of Economics* (New York: John Wiley & Sons, 1950), p. 135.

26. William W. Cochrane and Carolyn Shaw Bell, *The Economics of Consumption* (New York: McGraw-Hill, 1956), p. 10.

27. "The Present State of Consumption Theory: A Survey Article," *Econometrica,* Vol. 29 (October 1961):735.

Chapter 8

1. John Kenneth Galbraith, *Economics and the Public Purpose* (Boston: Houghton Mifflin Company, 1973), p. 112.

2. Carolyn Shaw Bell, *Consumer Choice in the American Economy* (New York: Random House, 1967), p. 378.

3. Cf. Robert O. Herrmann, "Consumerism: Its Goals, Organizations, and Future," *Journal of Marketing* (October 1970), pp. 55–60.

4. James E. Haefner and Steven E. Permut, "Indexing Consumerism Issues Through the Mass Media," *Journal of Consumer Affairs* (Summer 1975), pp. 81–89.

5. General Mills, *American Family Report 1974-75* (Minneapolis: General Mills, 1975), p. 53.

6. Nadel, *Politics of Consumer Protection,* pp. 36–41.

7. See, for example, Carlton P. McNamara, "Present Status of the Marketing Concept," *Journal of Marketing* (January 1972), pp. 50–57.

8. Sam Peltzman, "An Evaluation of Consumer Protection Legislation: The 1962 Drug Amendments," *Journal of Political Economy* (September–October 1973), pp. 1049–1091.

9. Peter H. Schuck, representing Consumers Union, quoted in *Congressional Digest* (November 1974), p. 284.

10. General Mills, *American Family Report 1974-75.*

11. David Hamilton, "What Has Evolutionary Economics to Contribute to Consumption Theory?" *Journal of Economic Issues* (June 1973), pp. 197–208, 206.

12. John Kenneth Galbraith, *The New Industrial State* (Boston: Houghton Mifflin, 1967), p. 216.

13. Cf. James S. Duesenberry, *Income, Saving, and the Theory of Consumer Behavior* (Cambridge: Harvard University Press, 1962).

14. Richard A. Easterlin, "Does Money Buy Happiness?" *The Public Interest* (Winter 1973), pp. 3–10.

15. Gerhard Scherf, "Alleviating Dissatisfaction," p. 65.

16. Daniel Bell, *The Coming of the Post-Industrial Society* (New York: Basic Books, 1973), p. 298.

Bibliography

Bibliography

Books

Aaker, David A. and George S. Day, eds. *Consumerism,* 2d ed. New York: Free Press, 1974.

American Council on Consumer Interests. *Proceedings of the 19th Annual Conference,* Columbia, Missouri: American Council on Consumer Interests, 1973.

Bell, Carolyn Shaw. *Consumer Choice in the American Economy.* New York: Random House, 1967.

Bell, Daniel. *The Coming of the Post-Industrial Society.* New York: Basic Books, 1973.

Berle, Adolf, A., Jr., and Gardiner C. Means. *The Modern Corporation and Private Property.* New York: Macmillan, 1932.

Boulding, Kenneth. *A Reconstruction of Economics.* New York: John Wiley & Sons, 1950.

Brainerd, J.G., ed. *The Annals of the American Academy of Political and Social Science,* Vol. 173 (May 1934). Issue titled "The Ultimate Consumer."

Campbell, Persia. *The Consumer Interest.* New York: Harper & Bros., 1949.
_____ *Consumer Representation in the New Deal.* New York: Columbia University Press, 1940.

Caplovitz, David. *The Poor Pay More.* New York: Free Press, 1963.

Chamberlin, Edward H. *The Theory of Monopolistic Competition.* Cambridge, Massachusetts: Harvard University Press, 1933.

Chase, Stuart and F.J. Schlink. *Your Money's Worth.* New York: Macmillan 1927.

Clark, Lincoln H. *Consumer Behavior.* New York: Harper & Bros., 1958.

Cochran, Thomas C. *The American Business System.* Cambridge, Massachusetts: Harvard University Press, 1965.

Cochrane, William W. and Carolyn Shaw Bell. *The Economics of Consumption.* New York: McGraw-Hill, 1956.

Coles, Jessie V. *Standards and Labels for Consumers' Goods.* New York: Ronald Press, 1949.

The Conference Board. *The Challenge of Consumerism.* New York: The Conference Board, Inc., 1971.

Consumer Behavior. Vol. 1. *The Dynamics of Consumer Reaction.* Sponsored by the Committee for Research on Consumer Attitudes and Behavior. Lincoln H. Clark, ed. New York: New York University Press, 1954.

Consumer Education: Why and How. Proceedings of a Conference on Consumer Education. George Peabody College for Teachers, May 1940. Nashville, Tennessee: George Peabody College for Teachers, 1940.

Consumer Federation of America. *Directory of State and Local Consumer Groups.* Washington, D.C.: Consumer Federation of America, January 1975.

Consumers Union of the U.S., Inc. *Consumer Education Materials Project.* Mt. Vernon, New York, 1973.

Council on Consumer Information. *Selected Proceedings of Annual Conferences,* 1957-1963. Greeley, Colorado: Colorado State College.

Cox, Edward Finch, Robert C. Fellmeth, and John E. Schultz. *The Nader Report on the Federal Trade Commission.* New York: R.W. Baron, 1969.

Dorfman, Joseph. *The Economic Mind in American Civilization.* Vols. 3, 5. New York: Viking Press, 1959.

Duesenberry, James S. *Income, Saving, and the Theory of Consumer Behavior.* Cambridge, Massachusetts: Harvard University Press, 1962.

Engel, James F., David T. Kollat, and Roger D. Blackwell, *Consumer Behavior* 2d ed. New York: Holt, Rinehart and Winston, 1973.

Esposito, John C. and Larry J. Silverman. *Vanishing Air: The Ralph Nader Study Group Report on Air Pollution.* New York: Grossman Publishers, 1970.

Galbraith, John Kenneth. *American Capitalism.* Boston: Houghton Mifflin, 1952.

―――― *Economics and the Public Purpose.* Boston: Houghton Mifflin, 1973.

―――― *The New Industrial State.* Boston: Houghton Mifflin, 1967.

General Mills. *American Family Report 1974-75.* Minneapolis: General Mills, 1975.

Green, Mark with Beverly C. Moore, Jr., and Bruce Wasserstein. *The Closed Enterprise System: Ralph Nader's Study Group Report on Antitrust Enforcement.* New York: Grossman Publishers, 1972.

Hamilton, David. *The Consumer in Our Economy.* Boston: Houghton Mifflin, 1962.

Hawley, Ellis W. *The New Deal and the Problem of Monopoly.* Princeton, New Jersey: Princeton University Press, 1966.

Hutt, W.H. *Economists and the Public.* London: Jonathan Cape, 1936.

Joint Council on Economic Education. National Commission on Economics and the Consumer. *Economics and the Consumer.* 1966.

Kallett, Arthur and F.J. Schlink. *100,000,000 Guinea Pigs.* New York: Vanguard Press, 1932.

Katona, George. *The Powerful Consumer.* New York: McGraw-Hill, 1960.

Kefauver, Estes F. *In a Few Hands.* New York: Pantheon Books, 1965.

Keynes, John Neville. *The Scope and Method of Political Economy,* 4th ed. Reprints of Economic Classics. New York: Augustus M. Kelley, Bookseller, 1963.

Kyrk, Hazel. *A Theory of Consumption.* Boston: Houghton Mifflin, 1923.

Linder, Steffan B. *The Harried Leisure Class.* New York: Columbia University Press, 1970.

Lynes, Russell. *The Tastemakers.* New York: Harper & Bros., 1954.

Mannes, Marya. *But Will It Sell?* Philadelphia: Lippincott, 1964.

Marshall, Alfred. *Principles of Economics,* 8th ed. London: Macmillan, 1947.

Mather, Loys L., ed. *The Economics of Consumer Protection.* Danville, Ohio: The Interstate, 1971.

McNeal, James U. *Dimensions of Consumer Behavior.* New York: Appleton-Century-Crofts, 1965.

Mendenhall, James E. and Henry Harap, eds. *Consumer Education.* New York: D. Appleton-Century, 1943.

Miller, Roger Leroy. *Economic Issues for Consumers.* St. Paul: West Publishing Company, 1975.

Mitchell, Wesley C. *The Backward Art of Spending Money.* New York: Augustus M. Kelley, 1950.

Nadel, Mark V. *The Politics of Consumer Protection.* New York: Bobbs-Merrill, 1971.

Nader, Ralph, ed. *The Consumer and Corporate Accountability.* New York: Harcourt Brace Jovanovich, 1973.

———— *Unsafe at Any Speed.* New York: Grossman Publishers, 1965.

———— ed. and Mark J. Green. *Corporate Power in America.* New York: Grossman Publishers, 1973.

National Association of Secondary School Principals. *Consumer Education in Your School: A Handbook for Teachers and Administrators.* Washington, D.C.: National Association of Secondary School Principals, 1947.

National Conference on Consumer Education. Proceedings of the First Conference. *Next Steps in Consumer Education.* Columbia, Missouri: Institute for Consumer Education, 1939.

National Conference on Consumer Education. Proceedings of the Second Conference. *Making Consumer Education Effective.* Columbia, Missouri: Institute for Consumer Education, 1940.

National Conference on Consumer Education. Proceedings of the Third Conference. *Consumer Education for Life Problems.* Columbia, Missouri: Institute for Consumer Education, 1941.

Norris, Ruby T. *The Theory of Consumer's Demand.* New Haven, Connecticut: Yale University Press, 1941.

Nourse, Edwin G., Joseph S. Davis, and John D. Black. *Three Years of the Argricultural Adjustment Administration.* Washington, D.C.: The Brookings Institution, 1937.

Packard, Vance. *The Hidden Persuaders.* New York: D. McKay, 1957.

Phillips, M.C. *Skin Deep.* New York: Vanguard Press, 1934.

Rainwater, Lee. *What Money Buys, Inequality and the Social Meanings of Income.* New York: Basic Books, 1974.

Robertson, Thomas S. *Consumer Behavior.* Glenview, Illinois: Scott, Foresman, 1970.

Robinson, Joan. *The Economics of Imperfect Competition.* London: Macmillan, 1933.

Schumacher, E.F. *Small Is Beautiful.* New York: Harper & Row, 1973.

Schlesinger, Arthur M., Jr. *The Age of Roosevelt I: The Crisis of the Old Order, 1919-1933.* Boston: Houghton Mifflin, 1957.

Schlink, F.J. *Eat, Drink, and Be Wary.* Washington, D.C.: Consumers' Research, Inc., 1935.

Scitovsky, Tibor. *Papers on Welfare and Growth.* Stanford, California: Stanford University Press, 1964.

Sheldon, Eleanor B., ed. *Family Economic Behavior: Problems and Prospects.* Philadelphia: J.B. Lippincott. 1973.

Slichter, Sumner. *Modern Economic Society.* New York: Henry Holt, 1928.

Smith, Adam. *The Wealth of Nations.* 2 vols. New York: E.P. Dutton, Everyman's Library, 1910.

Sorenson, Helen. *The Consumer Movement.* New York: Harper & Bros., 1941.

Strumpel, Burkhard, et al., eds. *Human Behavior in Economic Affairs.* San Francisco: Jossey-Bass, 1972.

Sutton, Francis X., et al. *The American Business Creed.* Cambridge, Massachusetts: Harvard University Press, 1956.

Swagler, Roger M. *Caveat Emptor!* Lexington, Massachusetts: D.C. Heath, 1975.

Thayer, V.T. *Formative Ideas in American Education.* New York: Dodd, Mead, 1965.

Till, Irene. *In a Few Hands.* New York: Pantheon Books, 1965.

Tonne, Herbert A. *Consumer Education in the Schools.* New York: Prentice-Hall, 1941.

Troelstrup, Arch W. *The Consumer in American Society,* 5th ed. New York: McGraw-Hill, 1974.

Veblen, Thorstein. *The Theory of the Leisure Class.* New York: Macmillan, 1915.

Wellford, Harrison. *Sowing the Wind: A Report from Ralph Nader's Center for Study of Law on Food Safety and the Chemical Harvest.* New York: Grossman Publishers, 1972.

Zwick, David and Marcy Benstock. *Water Wasteland: Ralph Nader's Study Group Report on Water Pollution.* New York: Grossman Publishers, 1971.

Articles and Periodicals

Aaker, David A. and George S. Day, "Corporate Responses to Consumerism Pressures." *Harvard Business Review,* November–December 1972, pp. 114–124.

Adams, Walter. "Consumer Needs and Consumer Sovereignty in the American Economy." *Journal of Business,* July 1962, pp. 264-277.

American Council on Consumer Interests. *Newsletter,* January 1974–September 1975.

Angevine, Erma. "The Consumer Federation of America." *Journal of Consumer Affairs,* Winter 1969, pp. 152–155.

Aranson, Peter H. "Federal Chartering of Corporations: An Idea Worth Forgetting." *Business and Society Review,* Winter 1973, pp. 59–64.

Armstrong, Richard. "The Passion That Rules Ralph Nader." *Fortune,* May 1971, pp. 144–147.

Barker, Solomon. "Trade Unions and Consumerism." *Journal of Economic Issues,* June 1973, pp. 317–321.

Bell, Carolyn Shaw. "Consumer Economic Power." *Journal of Consumer Affairs,* Winter 1968, pp. 155–166.

Boulding, Kenneth. "The Household as Achilles' Heel." *Journal of Consumer Affairs,* Winter 1972, pp. 110–119.

Bowman, Mary Jean. "The Consumer in the History of Economic Doctrine." *American Economic Review, Papers and Proceedings,* Vol. 41 (May 1951): 1–18.

Chandler, Charles C. "Consumer Education: Past and Present." *The Social Studies,* April 1974, pp. 146–150.

Congressional Digest, February 1971; November 1974.

Consumer Bulletin, 1935–1968.

Consumer Reports, 1936–1975.

"The Consumer—Another Forgotten American." Prepared by the Education Division of Consumers Union of the United States. *Social Education,* October 1974, pp. 498–532.

Darrow, Richard W. "Super Protection, Who Wants It?" Address, Television Bureau of Advertising, New York, November 15, 1967. *Vital Speeches,* January 1, 1968, pp. 171–174.

Drew, Elizabeth Brenner. "The Politics of Auto Safety." *Atlantic Monthly,* October 1966, pp. 95–102.

Easterlin, Richard A. "Does Money Buy Happiness?" *The Public Interest,* Winter 1973, pp. 3–10.

Eisner, R. *"Citizen Nader* by C. McCarry." *Saturday Review,* April 1, 1972, pp. 73–74.

Ferber, Robert. "Consumer Economics, A Survey." *Journal of Economic Literature,* December 1973, pp. 1303–1342.

———— "Research on Household Behavior." *American Economic Review,* Vol. 52 (March 1962): 19–63.

Fraser, Edie. "Consumer Legislative Update." *Business and Society Review,* Winter 1974–1975, pp. 58–63.

Friedman, Milton. *Newsweek,* Feburary 19, 1973, p. 70.

Greider, W. "How Far Can a Lone Ranger Ride?" *Ramparts,* March 1974, pp. 21–23.

Gould, Charles L. "Advertising." Address before a Conference of the Advertising Federation of America, Febriary 8, 1967. *Vital Speeches,* May 1, 1967, pp. 434–438.

Greyser, Stephen A. and Steven L. Diamond, "Business Is Adapting to Consumerism." *Harvard Business Review,* September–October 1974, pp. 38–58.

Gross, Susan. "The Nader Network." *Business and Society Review,* Spring 1975, pp. 5–15.

Hamilton, David. "What Has Evolutionary Economics to Contribute to Consumption Theory." *Journal of Economic Issues,* June 1973, pp. 197–208.

Harrod, R.F. "The Scope and Method of Economics," *Economic Journal,* Vol. 49 (September 1938): 383–412.

Haefner, James E. and Steven E. Permut. "Indexing Consumerism Issues through the Mass Media." *Journal of Consumer Affairs,* Summer 1975, pp. 81–89.

Herrmann, Robert O. "Consumerism: Its Goals, Organizations and Future." *Journal of Marketing,* October 1970, pp. 55–60.

Hogarty, Thomas F. "Survey of Non-Federal Consumer Protection Groups." *Journal of Consumer Affairs,* Summer 1975, pp. 107–113.

Houthakker, H.S. "An Economist's Approach to the Study of Spending." In Nelson H. Foote, ed. *Household Decision-Making. Consumer Behavior,* Vol. 4 New York: New York University Press, 1961.

———— "The Present State of Consumption Theory: A Survey Article." *Econometrica,* Vol. 29 (October 1961): 704–740.

"Is War on Poverty Becoming War on Business?" *Nation's Business,* March 1966, pp. 40–41.

Jones, Mary Gardiner. "Planning the Federal Trade Commission's Consumer Protection Activities." *Journal of Consumer Affairs,* Summer 1974, pp. 8–29.

Kyrk, Hazel. "The Development of the Field of Consumption." *Journal of Marketing,* Vol. 4 (July 1939): 16–19.

Lane, Sylvia. "Economics of Consumer Class Actions." *Journal of Consumer Affairs,* Summer 1973, pp. 13–22.

Lerner, Abba P. "The Politics and Economics of Consumer Sovereignty." *American Economic Review, Papers and Proceedings,* Vol. 62 (May 1972): 258–266.

"A Lesson from Cranberries." *Consumer Reports,* January 1960, pp. 47–48.

Lynd, Robert S. "Family Members as Consumers." *The Annals of the American Academy of Political and Social Science,* Vol. 160 (March 1932): 86–93.

———— "The Consumer Becomes a 'Problem'." *The Annals of the American Academy of Political and Social Science,* Vol. 173 (May 1934): 1–6.

Mack, Ruth P. "Economics of Consumption," in *A Survey of Contemporary Economics.* Bernard F. Haley, ed. Homewood, Illinois: Richard D. Irwon, 1952.

McCroskey, Jack. "An Optimist Looks at the Economy." *University of Denver Magazine,* Vol 4 (March 1967), pp. 16–18.

McNamara, Carlton P. "Present Status of the Marketing Concept." *Journal of Marketing,* January 1972, pp. 50-57.

Means, Gardiner C. "The Consumer and the New Deal." *The Annals of the American Academy of Political and Social Science,* Vol. 173 (May 1934): 7-17.

—— "The New Monopolies." *Consumer Reports,* April 1975.

Nader, Ralph. "Action for a Change." Ralph Nader, ed., *The Consumer and Corporate Accountability.* New York: Harcourt Brace Jovanovich, 1973.

—— "The Burned Children." In Nader, *The Consumer and Corporate Accountability.*

—— "The Case for Federal Chartering." In Nader, *Corporate Power in America.*.

—— "A Citizen's Guide to the American Economy." *New York Review,* September 2, 1971, pp. 14-18.

—— "The Free Market and Other Myths." *Business and Society Review,* Summer 1972, pp. 29-33.

—— "Nader on Nuclear Alternatives." *New York Times Magazine,* March 24, 1974, p. 8.

Nader, Ralph and Aileen Coward. "Claims Without Substance." In Nader, *The Consumer and Corporate Accountability.*

"Ralph Nader, The Man in the Class Action Suit." *Rolling Stone,* November 20, 1975, pp. 54-58.

Palmer, H. Bruce. "Progressive Enterprise." In *Business and the Consumer,* Washington: The American University, 1971.

Peltzman, Sam. "An Evaluation of Consumer Protection Legislation: The 1962 Drug Amendments." *Journal of Political Economy,* September–October 1973, pp. 1041-1091.

Peterson, Esther. "Consumerism as a Retailer's Asset." *Harvard Business Review,* May–June 1974, pp. 91-101.

Reynolds, Alan. "What Does Ralph Nader Really Want?" *National Review,* February 28, 1975, pp. 219–223.

Rothenberg, Jerome. "Consumers' Sovereignty Revisited and the Hospitality of Freedom of Choice." *American Economic Review, Papers and Proceedings,* Vol. 52 (May 1962): 269-283.

Rothman, Julius F. "How the AFL-CIO Helps to Inform Consumers." In Council on Consumer Information, *Selected Proceedings. Sixth Annual Conference,* Greeley, Colorado: Colorado State College.

Scherf, Gerhard W.H. "Consumer Education as a Means of Alleviating Dissatisfaction." *Journal of Consumer Affairs,* Summer 1974, pp. 61-75.

Seitz, Wesley, D. "Consumer Education as the Means to Attain Efficient Market Performance." *Journal of Consumer Affairs,* Winter 1972, pp. 198-209.

Tosdale, Harry R. "Bases for the Study of Consumer Demand." *Journal of Marketing,* Vol. 4 (July 1939): 3-15.

Uhl, Joseph N. "Consumer Education: Everybody Needs It."*American Education*, January-February 1971, pp. 13-17.

⸻ "The Purdue Consumer Education Study." *Journal of Consumer Affairs*, Winter 1970, pp. 214-234.

Warland, Rex H. Review of Barbara B. Murray, *Consumerism. Journal of Consumer Affairs*, Summer 1974, pp. 111-112.

Warne, Clinton L. "The Consumer Movement and the Labor Movement."*Journal of Economic Issues*, June 1973, pp. 307-316.

Whiteside, Thomas. *Profile* on Ralph Nader. *The New Yorker*, October 8, 15, 1973.

Public Documents

Colorado. Colorado Legislative Council. *Consumer Problems in Colorado*, Research Publication 112 (1966).

Colorado. Metropolitan Denver District Attorney's Consumer Office. *Year-End Report, March 1, 1974-February 28, 1975.* Mimeographed.

Consumer Action and the War on Poverty. Excerpts from Conference Proceedings. (Sponsored by Office of Economic Opportunity—Community Action Program and the President's Committee on Consumer Interests.) Washington, D.C. 1965.

Johnson, Lyndon B. "Special Message to the Congress on Consumer Interests, February 5, 1964." *Public Papers of the Presidents, 1963-64* Book 1. Washington, D.C.: Government Printing Office, 1965.

"Special Report." Memo from Esther Peterson to the President. "The Regional Consumer Conferences: Comments, Conclusions, Recommendations." n.d.

U.S. Congress. House of Representatives. Committee on Governmental Operations. *Hearings, Consumer Protection Activities of the Federal Departments and Agencies.* 87th Cong., 1st sess., 1961.

U.S. Congress. House of Representatives. Subcommittee of the Committee on Government Operations. *Hearings, Organizing Federal Consumer Activities.* Part 2. 91st Con., 2d sess., 1970.

U.S. Congress. House of Representatives. Subcommittee of the Committee on Government Operations. *Hearings To Establish a Consumer Protection Agency.* 93rd Cong., 1st sess., 1973.

U.S. Congress. House of Representatives. *Hearings Before the Special Committee to Investigate Executive Agencies.* 78th Cong., 1st sess., 1962.

U.S Congress. Senate. Committee on Banking and Currency. *Hearings, Truth in Lending.* 87th Cong., 1st sess., 1961.

U.S. Congress. Senate. Subcommittee of the Committee on Banking and Currency. *Hearings, Truth in Lending 1963-64.* 88th Cong., 1st sess., 1964.

U.S. Congress. Senate. Committee on Commerce. *Hearings on Fair Packaging and Labeling.* 89th Cong., 1st sess., 1965.

U.S. Congress. Senate. Subcommittee on Consumers of the Committee on Commerce and the Subcommittee on Representation of Citizen Interests of the Committee on the Judiciary. *Hearings, Consumer Controversies.* 93rd Cong., 2d sess., 1974.

U.S. Congress. Senate. Subcommittee on Reorganization, Research and International Organization of the Committee on Government Operation and the Subcommittee on Consumers of the Committee on Commerce. *To Establish an Independent Consumer Protection Agency.* Joint Hearings. 93rd Cong., 1st sess., 1973.

U.S. Congress. Senate. Subcommittee on Antitrust and Monopoly of the Committee on Judiciary. *Hearings Administered Prices.* Part 1, *Opening Phase— Economists Views.* 85th Cong., 1st sess., 1957.

U.S. Congress. Senate. Subcommittee on Antitrust and Monopoly of the Committee on Judiciary. *Hearings, Administered Prices.* Parts 9 and 10, *Alternative Public* Policies. 86th Cong., 1st sess., 1959.

U.S. Congress. Senate. Subcommittee on Antitrust and Monopoly of the Committee of the Judiciary. *Hearings, Packaging and Labeling Practices.* 87th Cong., 1st sess., 1961.

U.S. Congress. Senate. Subcommittee on Antitrust and Monopoly of the Committee on Judiciary. *Hearings, Administered Prices. A Compendium on Public Policy.* 88th Cong., 1st sess., 1963.

U.S. Department of Health, Education, and Welfare, Office of Consumer Affairs. *State Consumer Action, Summary '74.* (Washington, D.C.: Government Printing Office, 1975).

U.S. National Bituminous Coal Commission. The Consumers' Counsel. *Protection for Consumers of Bituminous Coal.* 1938.

U.S. Office of Consumer Affairs. *An Approach to Consumer Education for Adults.* Washington, D.C.: Government Printing Office, January 1, 1973.

U.S. Office of the President. Consumer Advisory Council. *First Report,* October 1963.

U.S. Office of the President. Consumer Advisory Council. *Consumer Issues '66.* June 12, 1966.

Index

Index

advertising, 16, 17–18, 19–21, 23, 24, 26, 27–29, 31, 33, 35, 44, 46, 63, 71, 80, 86, 88–91, 92, 97, 102, 105; bait and switch, 47; and Nader, 56–57, 62
AFL-CIO, 41, 73
Agency for Consumer Advocacy, 40
Agricultural Adjustment Administration (AAA), 24-25
agriculture, 24, 26, 33, 41, 55
Agriculture, Department of, 24, 25, 26, 39
Alabama, 46
American Association of University Women (AAUW), 27, 76
American Bar Association, 54
American Capitalism, 32-33
American Economic Association, 93
American Federationist, The, 73
American Home Economics Association, 76
American Telephone and Telegraph, 58, 101
American Veterans Committee, 32
antitrust, 59, 101
automobiles, 51–53, 60, 100
Automobile Safety Foundation, 52

"Backward Art of Spending Money, The", 12
Bell, Carolyn, 97
Bell, Daniel, 108
Bentham, Jeremy, 9
Berle, Adolf A., Jr., 17
Better Business Bureau. *See* National Better Business Bureau
Bituminous Coal Division, Department of Interior, 25
Boulding, Kenneth, 94, 108
bureaucracy, 104
Bureau of Mines, 53
Bureau of Reclamation, 54
business, 21, 24, 25, 28, 31, 33, 43, 55; conflict with consumer move-

ment, 28–29, 40, 62, 76, 80, 85, 89–91, 99–100; and Nader, 51, 62, 64–66
Business Week, 29

California, 49
Caplovitz, David, 80
Carnegie Foundation, 55
Center for the Study of Responsive Law, 55
Central Labor Union of Charleston, South Carolina, 32
Chamber of Commerce, 41
Chamberlin, Edward H., 17–18
Changing Times, 72
Chase, Stuart, 19–21
Cigarette Act of 1965, 39
cigarettes, 35, 39, 53, 101
Citizen Action Groups, 55, 70
Civil Aeronautics Board (CAB), 42, 58
civil rights movement, 46
class-action suits, 59–60
Coal Mine Health and Safety Act of 1969, 53
Coming of the Post-Industrial Society, The, 108
Commerce, Department of, 23, 26, 39, 58
Commerce, Secretary of, 38
"compensatory consumption," 102
competition, 8, 17–18, 26, 33, 35, 40, 42, 79, 81, 84–85, 89; and Nader, 57–60, 62, 67
Comprehensive Occupational Safety and Health Act of 1970, 53
Congressional Joint Economic Committee, 43
Congress Watch, 55
"conspicuous consumption," 11, 13, 85, 102, 106
consumer: defintion of, 83–84; and government, 35–42, 100-101
Consumer, Department of (proposed), 27, 33, 39

About the Author

Lucy Black Creighton is Associate Professor of Economics at Colorado Women's College in Denver where she has been teaching since 1964. She graduated magna cum laude from Smith College in 1949 and received the M.A. in economics from Radcliffe College in 1952. She wrote her doctoral dissertation, of which this book is a revised version, under the direction of Professor John Kenneth Galbraith. She was granted the Ph.D. from Harvard University in 1969. Dr. Creighton has served as research economist at the Denver Research Institute. She is currently a member of the Board of Directors of the Rocky Mountain Women's Institute in Denver and of the Board of Trustees of Smith College, Northampton, Massachusetts.